VODKA IN A
VEGEMITE JAR

An Australian on a
Soviet Antarctic Expedition

Trevor Hamley

First published in Australia in 2023 by Trevor Hamley

Email for correspondence: trevor.hamley@gmail.com

© Trevor Hamley 2023

ISBN 9780645855708 (paperback)
IBSN 9780645855715 (ebook)

NATIONAL LIBRARY OF AUSTRALIA

A catalogue record for this book is available from the National Library of Australia

Disclaimer

The author has made every effort to ensure the information in this book was correct at the time of publication.

All photos are the property of the author (with the exception of the image on p. 136 – 'A newsclip from the Soviet Union Illustrated Monthly' which was provided by Vladimir Papitashvili).

Serious work in exploration calls for as definite and as rigorous professional preparation as does success in any other serious work in life. Infinite harm has been done to the true profession of exploring by the entrance into the field of all sorts of people who have no proper place in it. Some of these people are mere adventurers looking for another thrill.

My Life as an Explorer by Roald Amundsen, page 237

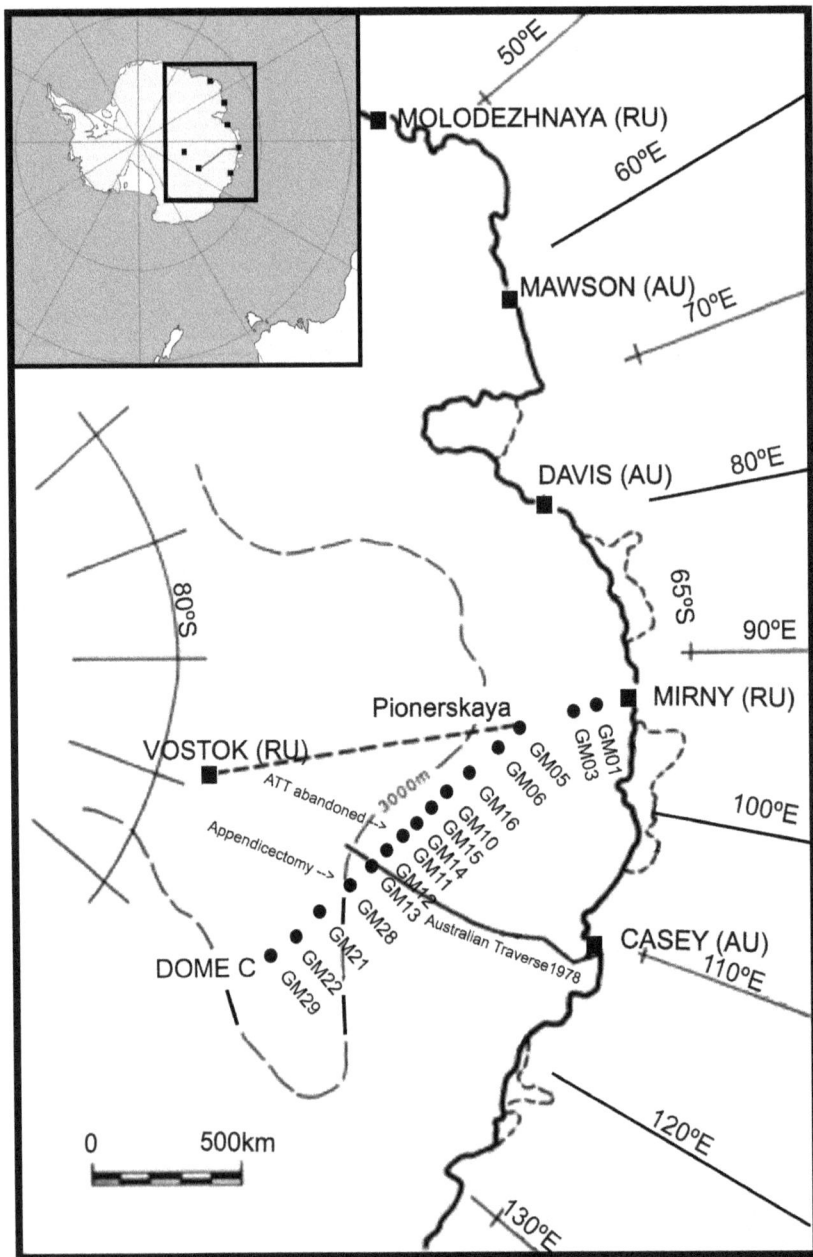

The traverse route from Mirny to Dome C

Contents

A Brief Guide To Reading This Book

YOREZ YONZF Just kidding

Please make allowance for Gaussberg, an extinct volcano 500km north-east of Davis on the West of Pazadowsky Bay. Just kidding.

I am Australian and this book is written with Australian spelling and language.

The five-letter codes shown under chapter headings followed by their meanings written in English are extracted from the 1982 Australian Antarctic Division (AAD)* Publication *Communicating with Antarctica Second Edition* ISBN: 0 642 887365. My extract (with meanings) is listed in a section at the rear of this book titled 'Communicating with Antarctica Decode section'. They comprise approximately 10% of the 576 codeword lexicon available at the time.

Antarctic terms and some Russian words and acronyms are marked with an asterisk when they first appear in the text, with their meanings defined in 'Antarctic Lingo' also a section at the rear of this book.

Chapters 1 to 3 provide context to my career as a glaciologist, including activities and experiences that preceded the Soviet expedition.

Chapters 4 and 5 go to the heart of this memoir. The narrative here is based on my journal recorded at the time. Chapter 4 covers the outbound route from Mirny (22 December 1983) to Dome C (2 February 1984). Chapter 5 covers the return route from Dome C to Mirny (10 March 1984).

Chapter 6 describes my time at Mirny after we returned from the traverse and waited to demobilise from the continent. Chapter 7 describes the extraordinary ship voyage home from Mirny to Fremantle. Chapter 8 delves into events that occurred subsequent to the expedition, in some cases years later. Chapter 9 looks back on my Antarctic experience from the viewpoint of the person I am today.

'Related Essays' expands on peripheral topics with a science twist.

The Story of Dr Leonid Rogosov concerns the doctor at the Soviet Antarctic station Novolazarevskaya, who in 1961 famously removed his own appendix.

Glaciology and Climate Change explores current scientific thinking about Arctic and Antarctic ice and climate change, in particular the state of balance of the East Antarctic Ice Sheet.

Author's Note

WYMMA

Please don't worry

I travelled to Antarctica in November 1983 to join a Soviet Antarctic Expedition (SAE) at the invitation of the Soviet Arctic and Antarctic Research Institute in Leningrad. My purpose: to participate in a three-month over-snow return traverse from the Antarctic coastal station, Mirny*, to a polar plateau highpoint named Dome C*, located near the South Geomagnetic Pole*. Our team of nine (including me), travelled in two tractor trains*, mostly following the 3,000 m elevation contour.

My glaciology career commenced in 1977, immediately after graduating from Monash University with a degree in civil engineering. I worked as a glaciologist for seven of my first 10 career years, including 12 months wintering* at Australia's Casey Station in 1978. During the latter stages of my glaciology career, I enrolled in a Master of Science degree from which I graduated in 1987.

Just nine months after being married in January '83, I found myself heading south onboard the Danish polar vessel *Nella Dan*, from Macquarie Wharf, Hobart, enroute to Mawson and thereafter by air to Mirny.

For three years between Antarctic expeditions (from 1980 to 1983) I worked at Barry's Beach Marine Terminal on the south-east coast of Victoria. I was, at the time, a fabrication engineer constructing Bass Strait oil and gas platforms. During this period I was informed by a previous glaciology colleague, that an imminent invitation was likely to arrive from Leningrad requesting, for the fifth and final occasion, an Australian glaciologist to join the Dome C team. I put my hand up immediately.

This is a memoir for posterity. My story in my words. A story that is entirely true, but my subjective truth. To protect privacy, some names and some sensitive numbers have been omitted or altered. Such amendments make no material difference to the story.

I began writing this narrative during the Covid-19 lockdowns after browsing my expedition journal for the first time since writing it. The Soviet expedition was a subject I rarely discussed over the years – other than glib remarks in after-dinner conversation. 'Yeah … I went to Antarctica twice, Casey for 12 months in '78, then with the Russians for five months in '83 … Yes, it was cold! Down to minus 60 … Yeah, that's correct … in '78 and again in '83 … I was the glaciologist! No, not glazier, glaciologist. Guess what, one of the blokes on the Russian traverse got appendicitis!' Then, someone would say something like, 'Isn't petrol expensive at the moment?' and the conversation would peter out. To explain what happened, to explain my involvement in the science of glaciology and to explain my connection with the SAE requires lengthy context. So, I might as well get on with it!

Antarctica is almost twice the size of Australia. Most people know it exists. Most people know it's cold and has something to do with climate change. Unfortunately, most people do not know much about Antarctic science. During the Heroic Age, Antarctic expeditions often purported a science objective to disguise ambitions for personal glory, national pride, profit, political advantage or all of the above. Who could cover the longest distance? Who could probe to the highest latitude and plant a flag? Who could find a better route to a given destination? Expeditions were mostly conducted by individual nations and funded by a combination of public and private sponsors. Sometimes the outcomes were far different from the objectives for which the funds were sourced.

Today, global travel companies are booming with customers interested in visiting Antarctica for a sensory experience, either by cruise ship or by aircraft. A traveller needs only the financial means. Satellite technology allows family and friends to track Antarctic voyages on their mobile phones. Social media facilitates communication with Antarctic locations at any hour of the day or night. The standard of accommodation on tourist expeditions is commonly five-star. My experience in 1983/84 was completely different, and rare!

In 2021, a comment I posted on the Facebook page of Absolute Antarctica led to a short article about my Russian experience. The positive feedback prompted me to preserve my journal electronically for family and friends. I quickly realised my scribblings were disjointed, poorly worded, repetitive and, in that state, not so interesting. The text required significant editing. I also wanted to include photographs. I attended one or two writers' workshops. My momentum gathered. I added chapters to explain events leading up to the expedition. I reflected on the human and social aspects of our journey, as well as our scientific achievements, including events that followed years later. I addressed questions I'd been asked over the years. How and why did I become a glaciologist? What were my qualifications and skills? How did the opportunity arise? Who did I know? Did I speak Russian? How did I get there? With each passing edit, my disjointed diary notes morphed into what I now think is a readable narrative.

Writing this book took decades to commence and six times as long as the expedition itself to complete. I was a glaciologist at the beginning of my career, but the bulk of my work life has been in commercial roles in the mining, oil and gas and civil infrastructure industries. My greatest challenge was the art of writing itself – not merely describing events – but relating events to the human experience of 'how it felt'; how I felt to be part of a foreign expedition in the world's most desolate, cold, barren and thoroughly alien landscape.

Background

YOSAZ YILAM

Polar Geography and Antarctic Life and Politics

I have been thinking. Would be glad of information concerning Polar Geography and Antarctic life and politics.

Polar Geography

The word 'arctic' derives from various roots: 'Arktos' in Ancient Greek and arcticus in Latin, meaning 'bear'. 'Bear' is a direct reference to the constellations Ursa Major (the great bear) and Ursa Minor, both pointers to the 'North Star' Polaris. Antarctica is the antonym of Arctic, an appropriate distinction etymologically, given the physical differences between the two areas. Both regions are cold and receive the same amount of sunlight. Both have a disproportionately large amount of frozen hydrogen hydroxide, or ice. Hydrogen hydroxide, or water as we usually call it, is unique. Water expands as it solidifies, unlike most compounds that shrink when they solidify. If not for this property, ice cubes in our drinks would not float. Fresh water freezes at zero degrees centigrade. Seawater freezes at -1.8°C.

The Arctic, or more correctly the area around the Geographic North Pole, is an ocean basin more than 4,000 m deep, covered by a layer of multi-year sea ice (frozen seawater). Antarctica is totally different. Antarctica is a continental land mass supporting a massive ice

1

sheet (frozen fresh water) shaped like an upturned bowl. The average elevation of Antarctica is 2,300 m above sea level: contrast that with Australia's average elevation of 330 m above sea level. At its deepest point, the Antarctic ice is 4,897 m deep, thicker than the deepest part of the Arctic Ocean, with a mean ice thickness excluding ice shelves of 2,126 m (Fretwell et al., 2013, p. 390).

Most of Antarctica lies within the Antarctic Circle, one of five major parallels that include the equator, the Tropic of Capricorn, the Tropic of Cancer and the Arctic Circle. By definition, the equator is at latitude 0°. The North and South Geographic Poles are at latitude 90°.

Antarctica is commonly described as the coldest, windiest, driest and highest continent on Earth. It is large and diverse with an area almost twice the size of Australia, equivalent to the combined size of the United States plus Mexico. Because of its size and geographic diversity, scientists typically divide Antarctica into three regions: East Antarctica, the smaller region of West Antarctica, and the smallest and most tourist-accessible region – the Antarctic Peninsula. East Antarctica contains the greater portion, compared with West Antarctica, of Antarctica's ice mass and land mass.

West Antarctica lies on the other side of the prime meridian and for convenience is usually demarcated from East Antarctica by the Transantarctic Mountains, which form a convenient physical boundary. Although covered by icesheet, approximately 45% of Antarctica's continental landmass is below sea level. In stark contrast, the Arctic sea ice forms over ocean and is surrounded by several continental landmasses including Eurasia, Greenland and North America, which acting together constrain the extent to which the Arctic sea ice can expand. Whereas the Antarctic Circle encompasses most of the Antarctic ice and land mass (but no countries), the Arctic Circle encompasses the northern extremities of numerous countries and territories including most of Greenland, large swathes of Russia, Canada and Alaska and a small part of northern Europe.

Greenland contains the largest ice sheet in the Arctic and lays claim to being the world's largest island, but it is also an autonomous country within the Kingdom of Denmark. Floating Arctic sea ice grows typically to a thickness of three to four metres during winter of which, on average, 40% remains through to the end of summer.

The Antarctic ice mass contains two-thirds of the planet's freshwater, if you consider all sources of freshwater including lakes, rivers, groundwater, glaciers and moisture in the atmosphere. The Southern Ocean is a key regulator of global climate through its interaction with the atmosphere, absorbing large portions of heat and carbon normally associated with climate change. It connects the world's major ocean basins, facilitating circulation and ventilating the deeper layers with surface layers of global ocean circulation. East Antarctic tabular icebergs* calve from ice shelves and glaciers at the ocean edge, floating away at the behest of coastal currents flowing opposite to the easterly direction of the circumpolar Southern Ocean current. Many floating giants run aground while passing over the continental shelf. They continue to melt, albeit slowly, while being splintered and smashed into smaller pieces by the effects of waves and tide. Some icebergs remain relatively intact until they gyrate into the circumpolar current. Once exposed to open ocean, calving, melting and fracture lead to rapid dissolution. Stresses produced by wave action, bend, flex and eventually fracture tabular icebergs. In a matter of months, icebergs born from continental ice hundreds of thousands of years old may be stripped of snow and tumbled into blocky cubes, splitting and rolling due to a shifting centre of gravity as they break up.

The Southern Ocean fractures tabular icebergs by wave action initially, producing pieces that are not only smaller but, due to the greater subsurface area, also melt faster per cubic metre than their tabular parents. So, although flexing caused by wave action is the initial dissolution process, melting soon takes over as the dominant dissolution process. Gradually but continually, small icebergs roll, calve and melt their way into remnants known as bergy bits* and growlers*, eventually melting away altogether. Generally speaking, Antarctic icebergs are goliaths compared with their Arctic cousins.

Antarctica is higher and less warmed by the ocean than the Arctic. It is therefore much colder, impacting the range of flora and fauna significantly. Antarctica is synonymous with numerous varieties of penguins, whereas no penguins live in the Arctic. The Galapagos penguin is one of the smallest and the most northerly species in the world. It lives and breeds all year round in the Galapagos Islands, right on the equator. The Arctic is synonymous with polar bears and arctic foxes, neither of which inhabit the Antarctic. Both regions provide friendly habitat for seals, whales and seabirds. Large areas of the Arctic are covered by lush, treeless tundras that support vibrant varieties of shrubs, mosses, grasses, lichens and flowering plants. In contrast, the Antarctic consists of one per cent exposed rock, the rest covered by ice, so plant life is less plentiful.

Many Indigenous groups live in the far north reaches of the Arctic. Humans, for example, are known to have inhabited Greenland for 4,500 years. Antarctica has never supported an Indigenous population. Humans are mostly found within scientific research stations, apart from the variety intent on trekking to outlandish destinations for notoriety.

Both the Arctic and Antarctic contain numerous 'poles'. The Geographic, or terrestrial, South Pole is the location commonly known as the South Pole. It is the point at 90°S made famous by the race to reach it in 1911/1912 between the Norwegian explorer Roald Amundsen and the British explorer Robert Scott. The Geographic South Pole is concentrically opposite the Geographic North Pole which, acting together, represent the points on the Earth's surface about which the Earth spins. The Earth spins with a small wobble that affects the precise location of the North and South Pole by a few metres at any point in time. The North Pole and the South Pole are approximately 10,000 km from the equator, the origin of a convenient definition for a unit of length. In 1791, the French Academie of Sciences implemented a proposal for a measurement of length (one metre) equal to one ten-millionth of the distance from the North Pole to the equator measured along a meridian passing through Paris.

The Earth's magnetic poles are generated by the internal magnetic field of the Earth's fluid core. The Magnetic Pole is the point on the surface of the Earth to which the compass needle points. In 1908, Douglas Mawson, accompanied by T.W. Edgeworth David, man-hauled from Cape Adare to a point on the Antarctic continent Mawson believed to be the location of the South Magnetic Pole at the time. Nowadays we know the precise location of the magnetic poles at both ends of the Earth. We also know these positions are shifting continuously. Today, the South Magnetic Pole lies off the coast of Antarctica not far from the French station at Dumont D'Urville and continues to move north towards Australia at a speed of 10 km to 15 km per year.

The lesser-known South Geomagnetic Pole* is also moving. Today it is located at latitude 80° 39'S, 107° 19'E, a distance of approximately 100 km from Vostok*. The study of the Earth's internal magnetic dynamo and its interaction with the interplanetary magnetic field is important for humans. The Earth's internal magnetic field shields life on Earth from harmful space radiation. Our closest planets Mars and Venus do not have an internal magnetic field and as such cannot protect life.

Another pole of renown within the Antarctic fraternity, but less familiar to the general public, is the Southern Pole of Relative Inaccessibility, defined as the location furthest from any point on the Antarctic coast. The Southern Pole of Relative Inaccessibility is considered the most remote point on Earth is and generally accepted as being located at or near the site of a now abandoned Soviet station (83°S, 55°E), marked by a plastic bust of Vladimir Lenin sitting atop a plywood tower attached to a balok*. It was established in 1958 during the International Geophysical Year at the same time Vostok was established. Cynics suggest it was positioned for political purposes! According to unconfirmed legend, the bust of Lenin was originally aligned to face Moscow but subsequently realigned to face Washington during a visit six years later by the US Antarctic Research Program.

The Arctic also has a pole of relative inaccessibility, but due to differences of regional geography, it is defined differently from its southern counterpart. The Northern Pole of Relative Inaccessibility is located at the point lying at the centre of a circle fitting entirely within the Arctic Ocean. This point was only defined with absolute certainty in 2013 following a review of satellite cartography. Due to the constant motion of the Arctic pack ice, no permanent structure can exist to mark its location. The best way to get to the Northern Pole of Relative Inaccessibility is by icebreaker – another example of how different the Arctic is from the Antarctic.

The East Antarctic Ice Sheet contains three major high points known as Dome A, Dome B and Dome C. Dome C lies within Australian Antarctic Territory and is located 560 km from Vostok. Dome C is particularly well suited to the study of astronomical sciences due to its elevation and mostly cloud-free atmosphere characterised by low dust and low aerosol content.

Antarctic Life and Politics

Modern living standards at Australian Antarctic stations compare favourably with an above average Australian mining camp. Expeditioners are well-rewarded financially, and certainly not unpaid, nor poorly paid, as they mostly were during the Heroic Age. Participation in the Australian National Antarctic Research

Expedition (ANARE)* offers adventure opportunities with minimal risk.

Once at a station, meal standards are exceptionally good. Internet browsing is usually available. Gymnasiums, recreation facilities, state-of-the-art vehicles, private sleeping quarters, libraries and pool tables are standard amenities. Some stations enjoy aviation support during summer months, removing much of the stress of emergency events. Australian Antarctic expeditioners enjoy armchair exposure to extreme weather events, exceptional views of aurora, spectacular sunsets, interaction with unusual wildlife, uncomplicated social responsibilities and a unique transit experience.

The lifestyle for an expeditioner in the field, away from the established stations, is very different. Accommodation is basic, and meals are self-prepared and unsophisticated. Modern amenities are totally absent. The routine is less predictable from day to day and at times dangerous. Out in the field, work hours are 24 hours a day, 7 days a week. Weather experiences can be life-threatening, although the privations are nowhere near as gruelling as those suffered during the Heroic Age.

For most expeditioners, the ambition to work in Antarctica begins as a bucket list objective. Some enjoy the initial experience so much they return again and again, hooked by the lifestyle, often building a career around a specialised science or a specialised profession or logistics skill. The opportunity to visit Antarctica as a guest of another nation is less common, particularly when the inviting nation has a spoken language and political ideology fundamentally different from your own. Expeditions are usually composed of homogenous groups from individual nations.

Numerous countries have probed Antarctica since the 1800s, perhaps even earlier, although sometimes 'science' is simply the pretext for mineral exploration. This, in part, may be because the icecap overlies a continental landmass known to be rich in mineral wealth. Early expeditions hoped to discover natural resources and/ or pursue territorial claims. In the early days, the idea of sharing Antarctic expeditions was abhorrent to the competing bodies funding them. Antonello (2018, p. 130) describes the earliest scientific plans developed at the inception of the ANARE from 1947, which emphasised meteorology and ionospheric research. Glaciology was not seen as 'economically promising or practically useful as other disciplines'. The initial task of ANARE was to effect administration of Australia's Antarctic possessions.

Global thinking about Antarctica has changed in the post– World War 2 era. Unlike other disputed territories, the world is savvy to the reality of Antarctic ownership claims and various national interests in mineral resources. During the International Geophysical Year of 1957/58, a movement emerged to treat Antarctica as a place of science – a demilitarised zone to be shared by all – in the common interests of all, and not as an area dominated or owned by individual nations.

The Antarctic Treaty, signed in 1959, enacted in 1961 by 12 nations (Argentina, Australia, Belgium, Britain, Chile, France, Japan, New Zealand, Norway, South Africa, the United States and the Soviet Union) and acceded to since by other nations, currently numbering 54, allows signatory nations the freedom to pursue scientific investigation and cooperation. The Treaty prohibits militarisation within both the continental and Southern Ocean areas. Seven sovereign states (Argentina, Australia, Chile, France, New Zealand, Norway and the United Kingdom) have made territorial claims within Antarctica, however, the Treaty, metaphorically speaking, has frozen those claims. Numerous countries, including China, Germany, India, Italy, Pakistan, Russia, South Africa, Ukraine,[1] and the United States, have constructed research facilities within areas

---

1. Vernadsky station was transferred by the United Kingdom to Ukraine in 1996 as an act of goodwill following the collapse of the USSR.

claimed by other countries. In 1983, the Soviet Union maintained more stations, more men (it was only men in those days), more ambitious science programs and a larger footprint in Australian Antarctic Territory than Australia itself.

Antarctica has always been a region of unparalleled political cooperation, due to the co-operation engendered by the *Antarctic Treaty*. The concern today is whether this co-operation will continue at the end of the 50-year *Protocol on Environmental Protection to the Antarctic Treaty* (the Madrid Protocol), which came into effect in 1998. The Madrid Protocol prohibits all activities relating to Antarctic mineral resources, except for scientific research. In coming years, the eyes of the world will be watching for signs of former 'scientific research stations' transforming into mining camps.

In 1997 Dome C became the location for a new joint scientific research facility named 'Concordia'. In 2005, Concordia commenced year-round operations, becoming the third permanent wintering-over research station on the Antarctic plateau, other than Vostok and the US Amundsen-Scott station located at the Geographic South Pole. Concordia is administered co-operatively by the French and Italian polar agencies, and maintained logistically from the French coastal research station Dumont D'Urville, located 1,100 km away.

CHAPTER 1

The Build-up

YORAD YOLYX YOURD

I have been very busy. Would like information about the Law Dome, an ice dome just over 1000m high to the south-east of Casey.

Why?

My ambition to visit Antarctica was triggered during a high school slide presentation by a physics teacher, who had wintered at Casey in the 1960s as an upper atmospheric physicist studying the aurora. I immediately decided to do something similar. Towards the end of my undergraduate university degree, I resurrected the idea and prepared a letter to the Australian Antarctic Division (AAD)*, requesting information on available roles.

A form letter arrived promptly, listing positions at four stations: Casey, Mawson, Davis and Macquarie Island. As I reviewed each job description, reality dawned.

Geez … I don't think I'm suited to most of these! Doctor … definitely not. Officer in Charge? … hmmm, I'm 23, not ready. Carpenter? Plumber? Electrician? … love to but I'm not a tradie … Meteorological observer? Radio technician? Diesel fitter? Cook? … no, no, no and no … but I do like cooking. Science jobs. Biologist? Well, umm … I don't think so. I don't really like biology and I'm a qualified civil engineer for goodness's sake. Then two more at the bottom. I know nothing about either, but my options are running out. Both sound interesting: upper atmospheric physicist? (no … no, there it is again?) and glaciologist? – both at Casey.

I considered applying to be the upper atmospheric physicist although I knew nothing about it. I just wanted to go south. Years later, I discovered that one of my colleagues who completed the Dome C traverse prior to me actually did commence his career as an upper atmospheric physicist. Never mind. This other role, 'glaciologist', seemed more aligned to my skills and interests. I could see myself as a glaciologist. *At least I can ski,* I thought, *perhaps being a Queen's Scout will help.*

My application for the glaciology position was the only employment application I submitted at the completion of my degree. I was thrilled when granted an interview from what I later understood to be an applicant field of 68. I considered my approach was unique at the time, but of course it had all been done before. The 24-year-old Norwegian Roald Amundsen, for example, was hired in 1896 by Adrien de Gerlache's Belgica expedition (the first to winter[*] in Antarctica) as a sailor before being promoted to first mate. This was the start of Amundsen's polar ambitions. Sancton (2021, p. 27) describes how Amundsen wrote to de Gerlache pleading, 'I have passed my middle school exams, the baccalaureate, and my navigation school exam' and am 'in good health'. Amundsen was physically strong, a good cross-country skier and did not expect to be paid. Who wouldn't be persuaded by such convincing and comprehensive reasons!

After an initial interview with the AAD Science Branch Head and the Personnel Manager, I progressed to a psych test and medical examination facilitated by the Department of Defence in St Kilda Road, Melbourne. I remember two things about the psych test. First, they seemed to ask the same questions over and over in different ways, which I found tricky when trying to second-guess the answer they wanted to hear. My other recollection involved remnants of a brief discussion I had with the examiner at completion. 'What exactly are you hoping to achieve?' I asked. 'Well, basically, we're trying to weed out unsuitable candidates' (oops).

By the time I graduated from Monash University in 1976, I was shortlisted but didn't have a written offer. I was 23 years old. During my graduation ceremony, I told friends about my likely employment as a glaciologist. A small group responded by hurling me semi-clothed into a fishpond near the Student Union building, then running off laughing. After working as a taxi driver for a few months, I finally received a written offer. I commenced with AAD as an Experimental Officer Grade 1 at the end of the first quarter of 1977.

How?

Australia is the only continent on Earth with no glaciers, and glaciology is a small fraternity globally. In Australia, education pathways and career opportunities are limited. Unlike trade roles, candidates for science positions in the AAD were not expected to have prior experience. A well-rounded applied science education, youthful exuberance, a flexible demeanour and the ability to cope with cold and remote climates were equally, if not more, important. Similar criteria applied during the Heroic Age, although back then it helped if you were one of the social elite: well-connected politically and independently wealthy, meaning you were willing to participate for free or donate money to fund an expedition.

At the time I commenced, the AAD Glaciology Section employed five permanent career scientists (plus another three or four casual staff not including expeditioners such as myself) under the leadership of Bill Budd – who later became the foundation Professor of Meteorology at the University of Melbourne. Bill was also my Master of Science supervisor. All the permanent staff had degrees in either maths or physics, each embedded in different research interests ranging from computer modelling to the flow law of ice. Some were interested in sea ice and its interaction with the ocean and climate. Others managed data-gathering expeditions to determine whether the Antarctic Ice Sheet was growing, shrinking or unchanging. Another program of intense long-term study involved ice core analysis, whereby sections of ice core were sampled and analysed by Australian and international laboratories using oxygen isotope techniques to determine past climate conditions. Thin slices of ice core cross-sections were also sampled and examined for crystal orientation to augment mathematical theories of ice sheet movement.

Glaciology expeditioners, typically numbering around six to eight, came from applied science backgrounds such as meteorology; civil, mechanical or electrical engineering; or surveying. The preferred skill profile depended then, as now, on details of the science program. Uwe Radok, one of Australia's pioneers in meteorological and glaciological research who headed the Meteorology Department as Reader in Charge at the University of Melbourne in the 1970s, was a qualified mechanical engineer (Antonello, 2018, p. 35; see also Houlden and Spark, 2022). Douglas Mawson is best known professionally as a geologist but started out as a mining engineer. He graduated from Sydney University in 1902 then resumed studies to complete a Bachelor of Science in 1905 before joining Ernest Shackleton in 1907 to 1909 (aged 25 years) as the expedition's physicist. Shackleton offered Mawson a wintering role for the duration of the expedition despite Mawson volunteering for a round trip only, essentially as a glaciologist. Mawson's stated objective was 'to see an icecap in being and become acquainted with glaciation and its geological repercussions' (Jacka and Jacka, 1988, p. xxvii).

Five of Mawson's nineteen fellow expeditioners on the 1911/12 expedition at Cape Denison were engineers (Jenson, 2015), of similar ilk to me. Mawson, a mining engineer, appointed 22-year-old civil engineer Earl Webb, who was also the last survivor of the Australasian Antarctic Expedition, as chief magnetician. He also appointed 24-year-old civil engineer (then employed by Queensland Railways) Edward Bage as astronomer, assistant magnetician and recorder of tides. Francis Bickerton, a 22-year-old mechanical engineer, was chosen to look after a Vickers aircraft that was converted to a device nicknamed 'the Grasshopper' (an aircraft with its wings removed) for towing sledges. Finally, 22-year-old Cecil Madigan, another of Mawson's appointments, became the meteorologist at Cape Denison after deferring his Rhodes Scholarship. He was a qualified mining engineer and the man chosen by Captain John 'Gloomy' Davis to lead the group who spent a second year at Cape Denison to search for Mawson, Ninnis and Mertz.

In the 1970s, expeditioners in wintering science roles were normally employed by the AAD on term contracts – in my case from early 1977 through to late 1979. ANARE expeditioners consisted of personnel from numerous organisations, the majority employed directly by the Antarctic Division. Light Amphibious Resupply Cargo (LARC) crews were seconded from the Australian Army. Helicopters, including air crews, were chartered from private enterprise. Most scientists joined or were seconded from government-funded research institutes and universities. Building trades personnel and science program affiliates often originated from collaborative government departments. Other team members such as artists or reporters, although fewer in number, joined the ANARE as the result of competitions, fellowships and publicity promotions.

In my day, the AAD fell within the administrative realm of the Commonwealth Government Department of Science, with its head office in St Kilda Rd, Melbourne. The Glaciology Section of the AAD occupied separate premises at the University of Melbourne. Our offices and laboratories were located within the Meteorology Department of the Earth Sciences School, Parkville, on the corner of Elgin and Swanston St, Carlton. Today, the AAD Head Office is in Kingston, Tasmania. The Glaciology Group is now located within the University of Tasmania campus in the Institute for Marine and Antarctic Studies (IMAS) building in Salamanca Place, Hobart.

My first year of full-time employment (1977 in Melbourne) prior to wintering in Antarctica (1978 at Casey) might be considered a form of paid internship where I learned by doing rather than through academic studies. I worked under the supervision of the returning 1976 Casey glaciologist. My university education refocussed as I dived into organising the arrangements and logistics of the glaciology program – to resurvey and extend an existing marker line further south into the area of Antarctica known as Wilkes Land. It was a year of high adrenaline during which expeditioners, including me, were provided with various preparatory training courses: outdoor survival, firefighting, plant operation, first aid and photography. Some expeditioners, particularly those not involved in fieldwork, had additional opportunities. The doctor, for example, was trained in basic dentistry. Several others received training as a surgical assistant.

Casey 1978

My year at Casey was a prequalifying experience for the Soviet expedition. In the 1970s and 1980s, Wilkes Land was an area of intense interest to Australian glaciologists. Over-snow 'traverse years' from Casey occurred every second or third year, interspersed with alternating years of ice core drilling on Law Dome, a small local ice cap about 70 km inland of Casey. Most scientific data collected by over-snow traverse occurred in spring when fine weather permitted safe travel deep into the Antarctic interior. Usually, a traverse during autumn set up fuel depots and rehearsed the logistics for a more ambitious program later in the year. Depending on the state of the mobile plant and the availability of personnel, a short winter traverse was sometimes conducted around the Law Dome.

In 1978, I spent 24 weeks participating in three inland traverses from Casey: six weeks on the autumn traverse, two weeks on a winter traverse, and sixteen weeks on the spring traverse. In spring we travelled directly inland, 900 km due south to latitude 74°S. We collected data in a team of three supported by a logistics team of three. Our work was part of a collaborative project known as the International Antarctic Glaciology Project (IAGP*). In 1979 I returned to Australia to spend the third and final year of my contract writing up results and handing over to the new team.

CHAPTER 2

Getting There

YADUZ YACAS fly

This is very urgent. Shall we endeavour to fly?

Science Objectives

The Mirny to Dome C traverse was part of the 29th Sovietskaia Antarktichekaia Ekspeditsai (Soviet Antarctic Expedition or SAE); the purpose was entirely scientific – to continue long-term field investigations into fluctuations of the magnetic field caused by the solar wind (plasma flow coming from the sun with an embedded interplanetary magnetic field) and its continuous interaction with the Earth's magnetosphere. The terrestrial study area extended from Pionerskaya, the site of an unmanned Soviet station, to Dome C – at the time, the site of a former unmanned US station. Both stations were abandoned when we passed through. This area is within the projection of the magnetospheric cusp region of the South Geomagnetic Pole down to the ionosphere and extends towards the so-called Corrected South Geomagnetic Pole.

The Dome C route was one of several, including Mirny to Vostok, that Soviet science teams had travelled almost every year since 1975. All were executed over similar distances but headed in different directions. Our path travelled west along an established route twice the distance of the typical Australian traverse of the time. Three Australian glaciologists preceded me on the Dome C route across four summer seasons: 1976/77, 77/78, 78/79 and 80/81. One colleague went twice. My one and only involvement (in 83/84) was the last in which an Australian participated and is likely to be the last for the foreseeable future.

The Australian/Soviet arrangement provided mutual benefits. For the Soviets it was a convenient way to obtain accurate coordinates of their automatic remote magnetic stations (ARMS*) using the emerging 'satellite navigation' technology developed by the Americans. For Australians, the traverse provided an opportunity, at minimal cost, to gather ice sheet movement data to be shared with IAGP participants – including the Soviet Union.

The ARMS measured fluctuations in the three components of the magnetic field, recording the data in analogue form on 35 mm film. Powered by an isotopic (radioactive) source, ARMS could function for 15 months between film canister changes. We carried a Geiger counter and, not unreasonably, some team members had safety concerns. The radio isotope generator consisted of less than one gram of Strontium 90 encased in 500 kg of lead, generating five watts of power and 200 watts of heat. Scientists and technicians from IZMIRAN – the Soviet Institute of Terrestrial Magnetism, Ionosphere and Radio Wave Propagation, incorporating the Polar Geomagnetic Research Laboratory – travelled to Antarctica annually to deploy and maintain the ARMS.

The Dome C traverse advanced the objectives of the IAGP in a section not otherwise accessed by dedicated glaciology investigations. IAGP ambitions for the overall study area included mapping the surface and bedrock topography to determine surface elevation and the thickness of the ice sheet, measuring the amount of snow gained on the surface versus the amount lost as meltwater and icebergs, and measuring structural and chemical properties of the ice.

My specific objectives were narrow: to simply (or not so simply as it turned out) finalise the remeasurement of slow-moving ice velocity markers that were established progressively since 1976/77. The exact location of some markers had not been remeasured. Others required further remeasurement. By establishing the location of a marker then remeasuring it later, the displacement calculated over the intervening period shows the surface ice movement rate – fundamental data required to calculate the mass balance of the Antarctic Ice Sheet.

The IAGP commenced in 1969 with a tentative 10-year timeframe and continued well into the late 1980s. The early years united research efforts by Australia, France, the United States, the Soviet Union and the United Kingdom, with the Japanese joining later. The IAGP collaboration area originally included the logistically accessible areas bounded by longitude 60°E to 160°E and from the Antarctic coast inland to latitude 80°S. The study area was expanded in 1980 all the way to latitude 90°S (the Geographic South Pole) and to longitude 20°E to incorporate Enderby Land in which the Japanese had commenced expeditions. Glaciology fieldwork conducted by ANARE during the early half of the 1970s, which also contributed to the IAGP, concentrated initially on ice movement across the 2000 m surface elevation contour in Enderby Land, and later on the ice movement flowline between the Casey and Vostok stations. Other activities included ice drilling investigations on Law Dome over a similar timeframe as the Soviet ice drilling activities at Vostok.

IAGP data formed a basis on which to derive mathematical models of ice sheet history aimed at predicting its future. The supporting field measurements included the precise location of ice movement markers using satellite doppler positioning equipment, barometric levelling to record incremental height differences between markers at satellite doppler stations, snow accumulation at the surface, radio echo-sounding through the ice mass to measure bedrock depth, gravity meter readings and the collection of shallow core snow samples for chemical testing. Collection of gravity data was considered valuable in the 1960s and early 1970s; it facilitated determination of ice depth at locations between the more coarsely spaced seismic soundings. Gravity data also interested geophysicists studying the 'gravity anomaly', helping them to interpret features of the basal crust under the ice mass. By the late 1970s, a 100 MHz 'ice radar'* supplanted gravity measurements as the preferred and more accurate method to determine ice depth. Glaciologists continued to record gravity but only as a fallback option should performance problems develop with the emerging technology. The gravity meter was small and simple to use but also delicate and expensive. It relied on a creeping spring mechanism. The data were easy to gather but not easy to interpret. By the early 1980s measurements were no longer routine on over-snow traverses.

New traverse lines were marked with a snow pole or cane marker every two kilometres. This enabled return travel by visual navigation in fine weather, or by radar during whiteout. It also facilitated the calculation of surface snow accumulation by measuring, then at a later date remeasuring, the height from the snow surface of a tag placed on the marker pole. The change in height for the time period between measurements revealed the snow accumulation rate. IAGP activities such as ice core drilling continue today, even though the original objectives have been long since achieved. Data gathering for mass balance calculations is now dominated by satellite remote sensing. Over-snow traverses for purely scientific purposes are largely unnecessary, other than to support drilling programs or to calibrate snow accumulation rates and surface snow density studies.

Preparations in Australia

Previous glaciologists to visit Mirny offered me practical advice before departure: 'It's unlikely anyone will speak fluent English. You certainly can't count on it! You will need to learn Russian.' 'Fantastic,' I said, 'I can't wait to get started.' The opportunity to participate in a Soviet Antarctic Expedition (SAE) appealed to me for many reasons.

In 1974, as a 20-year-old engineering student I travelled alone across Russia on the Trans-Siberian Railway during my deferred third year at university, an adventure that was challenging to organise, and expensive. At the time I could find only one travel agent in Melbourne capable of booking the arrangements. As a music student at high school, I loved trad jazz and still do, none more so than Kenny Ball whose chart-topping 1961 hit 'Midnight in Moscow', written in 1955 with the original title 'Leningrad Nights', was renamed 'Moscow Nights' at the request of the Soviet Ministry of Culture. It is also known as Moscow Suburban Evenings. A simple but exquisite example of the richness, contradiction and complexity between Russian arts, science, culture, and politics.

During my six-month preparations in Australia in mid-1983, prior to departure for the SAE I did little else other than read, write and practice Russian: a daunting but exciting task. I knew I could only achieve an elementary understanding of the Russian language. My employer arranged and paid for private tuition at the Russian Department of the University of Melbourne. Once a week I traipsed across the campus to be guided through structured tutorials and exercises and then continued my studies after hours. Most of my learning came from a textbook, *Mastering Russian*, that I took with me to Mirny. To reinforce private tuition, I also attended Russian 101 lectures with the knowledge and approval of the language school.

I purchased several dictionaries. The most informative was a two-volume Russian–English and English–Russian dictionary that was too bulky to carry. I also purchased a pocket dictionary that I carried everywhere. Studying Russian demanded concentration, memory and manipulation of the tongue-twisting pronunciations of the Cyrillic[2] alphabet of 32 letters.

I made a tactical mistake with my tutor by admitting I studied German at high school. My tutor would say far too often, 'You should

---

2. Means derived from Greek.

have a good head start having studied German at high school!' and 'The similarities between Russian and German grammar should make things easier for you.' Oh dear! I absorbed her encouragement in silence. My confidence was crushed one day when I met a younger student studying three languages at once (apparently successfully), including both Russian and Chinese. This struck me as both awe-inspiring and depressing. My tutor 'explained me' (sic) the differences between English and Russian. 'Russian is difficult to learn initially,' she would say, 'but become easier when you understand … grammar. Only one way to say something in Russian. English on other hand, is easy at start, but difficult to master.' We discussed inconsistencies in spelling and the complexity of English versus Russian grammar. We also discussed English words with similar meanings, or similar sounding words with different spellings, that make English challenging as a second language. How many native English speakers, for example, could explain or provide an example of a homophone, homograph and homonym without first consulting a dictionary?

In English, you may deliver a string of words in almost any order and convey meaning. You may also convey meaning with incorrect spelling, omitted pronouns, mixed tenses and incorrect grammar. The same cannot be said or communicated effectively with Russian. Russian is binary. Either you understand, or you don't understand. I fell into the latter category most of the time. I struggled to memorise words and phrases, and the method for conjugating verbs. One handy tip from my tutor involved Russian words starting with 'a'. 'These commonly derive from English,' she said. As an English speaker, if you can pronounce the Russian alphabet phonetically, you will recognise Russian words commencing with 'a'. For example, knowing that in Russian, the letter 'p', pronounced phonetically, sounds like 'r', and 'k', 't' and 'e' have the same pronunciation as English, the meaning of the Russian word 'aktep' should be obvious. The meaning of the Russian word 'atom' is even more obvious.

I found Russian far more difficult to read than speak. With Latin languages, for example Spanish, it tends to be the other way around – easier to read than speak. Perhaps this is because Latinos speak fast and slur their pronunciation. With Russian, I could read snippets of newspapers or magazines, but was never capable of reading books.

Apart from the challenge of communicating face-to-face in Antarctica, a separate challenge involved the methods by which I might communicate from Antarctica to both work colleagues and my wife in Australia. With no access to telex* machines or 'radphones'* (radio phones) out in the field, the obvious solution was amateur radio, but I didn't have a licence! I approached the regulatory authority of the day (the Post and Telecommunications Department) to plead my case for an exemption from a morse code test and radio theory test, and the Department cooperated; I was granted a 'limited licence', after which the AAD sourced and equipped me with an Astro C, military-spec high frequency radio. This added significant bulk and weight to my growing cargo which already included two JMR*-brand, second-generation global positioning system (GPS) units.

The JMR was a ground-based receiver of US Navy navigation satellite signals for measuring surface position coordinates in mapping and surveying tasks. My JMRs were amongst the first owned and used by a non-military organisation in Australia. My primary unit (s/n JMR-004) was owned by the AAD. The Division of National Mapping (another Commonwealth department) supplied a second unit on loan (s/n JMR-1).

The prospect of joining the Soviet expedition thrilled me. My wife was less thrilled. Leaving Australia before our first wedding anniversary did not align with Kerry's marriage expectations. Some of Kerry's work colleagues and relatives also did not share my excitement and expressed this to Kerry. And then, on 1 September 1983, just months before my scheduled departure, Soviet forces shot down

Korean Airline Flight 007 over the Kamchatka Peninsula in Russia's far east. I thought my plans were also shot down.

The Korean Airline incident was an atrocious act. The political fallout was huge. I waited for weeks wondering whether my trip would be cancelled. Ultimately, just like trickle-down economics, the international ructions I feared did not trickle down. I was issued with an Australian diplomatic passport and advised verbally to proceed. Australian expeditioners do not normally need a passport. Visits to foreign Antarctic stations by Australian citizens or ships are only subject to commonsense protocols such as requesting and being granted permission from the station's officer in charge (OIC*). A diplomatic passport was issued to me as a precaution. Should I need to disembark at an unfriendly international location on the return voyage to Australia, it would expedite customs and immigration arrangements for both me and my accompanying boxes of expensive (and potentially suspicious) equipment.

At that time, Ronald Reagan had proposed the Strategic Defence Initiative (SDI) – colloquially labelled Star Wars, a system of 'yet to be developed' technology intended to intercept and prevent a nuclear missile attack on the US by the Soviet Union. The SDI was eventually abandoned at the end of the Cold War before anything was completed. That same year, the US also sent its first woman into space, Sally Ride. Although rightly celebrated by the West, 20 years earlier the Soviet Union had already sent its first female cosmonaut – the 26-year-old Valentina Tereshkova – on a solo space mission to circle Earth 48 times aboard Vostok 6.

When I departed Australia for Mirny, we had no definitive plan for my return. The itinerary and logistics depended on the date of our return to Mirny from the traverse, and the quirky irregularities of Antarctic resupply voyages. I only knew that I could not (and would not) depart Mirny by air, in a reverse of the logistics by which I arrived. By the time we were forecast to have returned from the traverse, flying operations out of Mirny would have ceased and would not recommence until the following spring.

I would eventually depart by ship, but when and by which voyage was unknown. Polar voyage schedules are unpredictable at the best of times due to the vagaries of weather, sea ice conditions, logistics priorities, science priorities, medical emergencies and unforeseen accidents. One of my predecessors departed Mirny by ship and disembarked to fly home to Australia on a commercial flight from the Canary Islands. Another disembarked when the ship was almost back to Russia.

The Voyage South

My journey to Mirny from Hobart began when I boarded *Nella Dan* on Monday 21 November 1983 at Macquarie Wharf for a two-week voyage to Mawson. From Mawson I was to be collected by a Russian ski-equipped aircraft and flown to Mirny, located due east and midway between the Australian stations Mawson and Casey. At 75 metres long with a speed of 12.5 knots and a passenger capacity of 42, *Nella Dan* was a petite polar vessel yet one of the longest continuously serving Antarctic ships of all time. Kerry was shocked to see her, particularly when I walked *down* the gangplank to board, admittedly at low tide. For Kerry, this was an omen that I may never return!

In most respects our voyage was no different from any other Australian Antarctic voyage, except that my destination was radically different from other passengers. Once on board, criss-crossing streamers connected passengers with a myriad of loved ones on the wharf. A sea of brave faces and flowing tears presented a confronting sight for partners at opposite ends of the streamers. The noise of *Nella*'s engines firing up and black smoke billowing from the funnel signalled imminent departure along with a crescendo of shouting and waving. The final moments were emotional. Fond farewells echoed back and forth, accompanied by the discordant ruckus of clicking cameras. *Nella* sounded the foghorn in a lengthy blast as we nudged off. Well-wishers jogged down the wharf as the vessel gathered speed. Everyone waved furiously and clung to the streamers until, finally, they broke. Family members and expeditioners burst into tears spontaneously. Kerry says she can't remember any streamers. I think she was stunned.

We sailed slowly down the Derwent River, an occasional blast from the ship's horn signalled our position: a loud, rich, resonating sound that spanned the waterway from Bellerive on our left to the central business district and suburb of Sandy Bay on our right. A poignant moment for individuals onboard, but a routine affair for Hobart's seafaring community, who have hosted Antarctic sailings for more than a century, dating back to the 1890s. Kerry says she cried all the way back to Melbourne. Most of the passengers on her afternoon flight were wives or partners of Antarctic expeditioners, many of whom were upset and teary during the flight, just like Kerry. Some were angry. A lady in the airplane seat next to Kerry subsequently gave Kerry a ride from Melbourne Airport to my parents' place in North Balwyn, where Kerry picked up our car and drove home alone to Mt Eliza.

Nella Dan was not a powerful icebreaker like the contemporary vessels *Aurora Australis* and *Nuyina*. *Nella*'s round hull broke pack ice by riding up on ice floes then used the ship's dead weight to crack them apart. Sometimes *Nella* would need to reverse and ram floes for hours and days on end without making headway. Ramming consumed copious amounts of fuel. It was effective but tedious and came with a major disadvantage at sea – the round hull facilitated ferocious roll. Ocean swells were not kind to passengers or crew vulnerable to seasickness.

Both *Nella Dan* and her older Danish sibling *Thala Dan* would pitch and roll with metronomic precision after leaving the calm waters of Port Phillip Bay or the Derwent River. Within hours the ship's deck was usually devoid of passengers. Many headed straight to their cabin to wedge themselves into a bunk, not to be seen until the ship reached the sea ice. Those worst affected could shed kilograms in a single voyage, the result of constant retching and lack of appetite. For some, the voyage experience was debilitating, with seasickness an unavoidable scourge despite the availability of preventative tablets and patches.

However, passengers able to attend meals enjoyed a wonderful experience. A typical breakfast menu (half in English and half in Danish) included juice, preserved fruit, marmalade, cereals, honey, grilled lamb brains, fried *codre*; eggs fried, boiled, scrambled or in an omelette; plus bacon, toast, milk, tea, coffee, rolls and toast. For lunch, *barquettes jardiniere*; boiled breast of beef with broccoli, corn kernels and *pommes bouillon*; cheese and biscuits; and tea, coffee, wine, beer and soft drink. A typical dinner menu was *potage cerfeuil*, *boeuf raifort avec salade*, mixed vegetables and baked potatoes, *patisserie*, cheese and biscuits, and tea, coffee, wine, beer and soft drink.

Ocean crossings in light seas and slight swells were bad enough, but when the 'Dan' ships encountered a Southern Ocean squall, the impact on passengers could be terrifying. As ocean winds increased, so did the howl of vibrating rigging, like strummed guitar strings. The little ship would shudder and shake from bone-jarring impacts with steep waves. Gale-force winds transformed the ocean into a washing machine of white water and foam. Foamy spray peeled from the highest waves, streaming water like a burst fire hose. Some waves sent a plume of spray right over the top of the ship. For the occasional passing albatross, violent seas were a playground of micro-lift to exploit by skimming wave crests. For humans prone to seasickness, it was a living hell. In heavy seas, pitch and roll were uneven and unpredictable, often causing *Nella* to roll 45 degrees to either side of vertical. Gigantic waves occasionally dumped swimming pool loads of water on the foredeck, often enough to ensure you did not want to be out there. Overspray and foam crashed, smashed and drenched both the ship and cargo, dislodging all objects and persons not tied down. The windscreen wipers on the bridge worked overtime just to maintain line of sight. In following seas, the ship would routinely rise to the crest of a wave, then surf down the other side and plough into the next wave like a submarine. Hardy crew members were often confined to bunks. I frequently discovered I was the only person moving around in the corridors and covered decks.

As we approached the Antarctic coast, the increasing presence of sea ice dampened ocean swell. The sea surface calmed, often to the point of dead calm. The ship's motion settled to the gentle, floating feel of a European river barge. Passengers affected by seasickness emerged quickly from their cabins, hungry and desperate for fresh air and exercise, and the sights of magnificent Antarctic scenery. We arrived at the sea ice edge, 35 nautical miles from Mawson, on 6 December 1983. The crew secured Nella using heavy, braided mooring lines tethered to land anchors driven into the sea ice one hundred metres away. We didn't move for the first two days while 50 knot winds, gusting to 70 knots, raged and howled. Unloading was prohibited. The ship held fast while we waited for improved weather to allow safe flying.

Thursday 8 December 1983:

I woke at 6:00am when the deputy voyage leader banged on my cabin door to ask if I could assist with the marshalling of expeditioners and their bags. The first task required flight crew to reassemble the helicopters by attaching the rotor blades then removing covers and tie-downs.

The first helicopter took off for Mawson at 7:30am carrying the voyage leader and sacks of mail. Inbound and outbound personnel boarded at the ship's helipad. For the remainder of our time at the ice edge, all cargo movements to and from Mawson were coordinated from the sea ice surface. The ship's davit cranes lowered inbound cargo onto the ice where boxes and crates were weighed manually, then manhandled into cargo nets. Each chopper would hover two metres above the surface while a loadmaster attached a cargo net to the underside hook. The loadmaster would then step away and give a thumbs up signalling clearance to leave. Choppers assigned to freight operations only landed on the ship to refuel.

When the wind ceased, the feeling out at the ice edge was tranquil and scenic. Passengers could wander on the sea ice and take photos provided they remained near the ship. Curious penguins would appear en masse, launching themselves out of the water like a missile attack, belly-skidding then flipping upright in one seamless motion. These happy, clean, odourless and photogenic creatures compared favourably to their stinky little guano-covered cousins I later experienced at nesting rookeries. They also seemed comfortable posing for photos although, being wild creatures, they never willingly allowed humans within touching distance, wary I'm sure of becoming possible sources of food. During the late afternoon and early morning, the low-hanging sun cast long shadows over otherwise invisible textures of the sea ice. The pastel colours of the ice and sky contrasted beautifully with the bright red hull of the ship. Long shadows, plentiful wildlife and rich ultramarine hues of the deep ocean created boundless subject matter for creative photographers.

Eventually my turn arrived for the short but exciting chopper transfer. I landed at Mawson at 7pm, fatigued and sleepy, then sat in the club until 1.30am to share a drink and stories with members of the outgoing crew while waiting for the radio sked'* with Molodezhnaya. Although keen to advise the Soviets of my arrival at Mawson and readiness to be collected at an hour's notice, luckily, I didn't hold my breath.

Mawson

Friday 9 December 1983:

I didn't know what to expect nor how long I'd be waiting. Mawson radio operators maintained regular contact with Molodezhnaya, but translation difficulties and local priorities slowed the information exchange. Our respective officers in charge at both Soviet and Australian stations co-ordinated and vetted messages. At 3:30pm I managed to contact Kerry successfully by radphone. We spoke for all of 5 minutes.

Initially I occupied myself by interacting with other scientists. My equipment remained fully packed. I also wandered around the station taking photos and occasionally helping to unload boxes. My conversation with Kerry, although I couldn't know it at the time, was the first of only a few direct discussions I had with her during the entire time I was away.

Saturday 10 December 1983:

I realised I may be waiting for an extended period. I therefore offered my services as a trades assistant to the crew building the Red Shed (the main accommodation building) and assisted 'Animal' with the plastering of the interior walls.

A short trip to the melt-lake during the early afternoon caused delay to a sked with my amateur radio buddy Earl in Frankston. Fortunately, propagation conditions were good and the call went ahead. Kerry hurried over by car from our home in Mt Eliza, arriving within twenty minutes. Kerry and I talked for 75 minutes about the usual things: a possum falling down the chimney, mechanical problems with our car, building activities in the street, the composition of dinner last night, the voyage on *Nella Dan* and, of course, the weather. I was sunburnt from the sunny weather at Mawson but Kerry had more significant problems to relay, concerning the 'possum'. It made a huge mess inside the house. Our obliging next-door neighbour came over to help Kerry remove it. One of my first jobs after returning from Antarctica was to install a chimney cap weathervane.

Sunday 11 December 1983:

I travelled out to Welch Island with a group of summer expeditioners to visit a penguin rookery. We crossed the sea ice on a selection of vehicles including three Odyssey go-karts, two skidoos with a trailer behind each, a three-wheeler Honda and a four-wheeler Suzuki rough terrain bike.

Monday 12 December 1983:

I continued to assist the carpenters install ceilings in the ground floor of the Red Shed. A telegram arrived from Molodezhnaya written in capitals, as follows:

TO MAWSON STATION DR T. HAMLEY

WOULD YOU PLEASE BE WAITING THE ANSWER FOR A SOME TIME STOP THE QUESTION OF YOUR DELIVERY TO MIRNX (sic) IS NOW DISCUSSION WITH OUR AVIATION STAFF STOP THE BEST WISHER, L BOULATOV, LEADER OF THE 29 SAE

Weather conditions were nauseatingly perfect. The days dragged as I continued to wait. Air temperatures hovered around zero.

Tuesday 13 December 1983:

I contacted Earl at 0900 Greenwich Mean Time to arrange a sked, for the following Saturday.

Wednesday 14 December 1983:

Still no news from the Soviets.

The guys at the station were also curious; Had I heard anything yet? When was I moving out? I posted the telegram received two days earlier from Molodezhnaya on the mess noticeboard. I didn't know it at the time, but one cause for the delay was the station leader at Mirny seeking formal permissions from Leningrad. What else could I do but eat! Morning tea offered a selection of pastries: yeast buns, vanilla slices, mint slices, cream biscuits, chocolate cake and fruit cake. I didn't hold back and noted in my diary: *'I'm probably putting on weight'*. Given the diet waiting for me over the next few months I shouldn't have worried. The food at Mawson was amazing. Trout for lunch, followed by a dinner of roast chicken with a plentiful dessert of caramel custard, apple pie and ice-cream. After dinner I went for a walk onto the sea ice. I was fortunate to hitch a ride on a quad-bike to Béchervaise Island where we checked out a small rookery of Adelie penguins. The location provided wonderful views of icebergs and mountains in almost every direction.

> *Thursday 15 December 1983:*
>
> *After dinner, an announcement boomed over the station public address system as I prepared for another penguin excursion. It called me to the radio room where I bolted like a racehorse. The OIC had news. According to the radio operators, as best they could understand, a special flight would leave Mirny at 2am Mawson time. The Soviets should arrive the following morning, just after breakfast.*

Over-excited by this development, I stupidly decided to proceed with the penguin excursion. I often ask myself in retrospect, why? And the best I can say is that it seemed like a good idea at the time. I considered that this would be my last opportunity to experience the sights, sounds and smells of a large nesting rookery – a unique and special experience.

Eight of us headed out onto the sea ice on a collection of trikes, quadbikes and go-karts. I was towards the rear of the group when a companion in front riding a small go-kart suddenly executed a four-wheel drift without looking or considering the consequences for following vehicles. I watched in horror as he came to a halt directly in my line of travel, by which time I was about 50 m away. I braked hard but could not slow down. I certainly couldn't dodge him. I skidded uncontrollably and piled into him at speed, rocketing straight over the handlebars. The stupid part is that I had a premonition of an accident just minutes before it happened.

In those days we didn't use, nor value, the use of personal protective equipment. I wore a beanie but no helmet. During the microseconds in which I flew over the handlebars all I could think was d*on't damage the camera in my backpack ... pleeeease don't damage the camera.... Please don't ...* then pause ... fly ... baaang! Hitting the ice was like smashing into concrete. I crashed like a ragdoll, then rolled and rolled and skidded. The adrenaline kicked in as I picked myself up, sore and dizzy. I remember rotating my head and neck and stretching my back before removing my daypack to check the camera. The top was slightly dented but the camera itself appeared to be working, a bit like me. My colleagues rushed over, visibly shocked. I was sore, but I thought I was okay. Clearly, they didn't. 'We need to turn around and get back to the station immediately. You need to see the doctor!' I raised a hand to the top of my head and understood immediately. Ahhh shit! I felt warm liquid, yep, blood, and lots of it. We hurried back. My colleagues radioed ahead to alert the doctor.

On arrival, I jogged straight to the surgery. The doctor cleaned my wound, inserted seven stitches in the crown of my head and filled me with painkillers and anti-inflammatories. He ordered me to remain in the surgery until midnight. Several colleagues called in to check on me. Groggy and bruised with a throbbing headache, a black eye emerged within hours. On edge and unable to sleep, I rose at midnight to finish packing personal effects. I worked alone, slightly wobbly, to move personal gear from my room to the tray of the utility truck in the equipment workshop – preparations I should have completed earlier in the evening. At 2am Mawson time, the radio shack received confirmation. The Soviets were in the air and on their way. Suddenly, the activities of the day caught up with me. I fell asleep totally exhausted, just when I should have been most alert. Throbbing head pain prevented more than a few hours of fitful rest. After breakfast, a group of around 20 accompanied me to the sea ice landing zone to wait for the arriving aircraft.

Landing airplanes, ski-equipped or otherwise, on ungraded sea ice is risky and far from ideal. Repeated messages from the Mawson OIC to Mirny offered fuel and assistance with arrival arrangements, but went unanswered. Mawson wintering personnel were proactive and marked out a landing zone in Kista Strait where the ice was least dappled and least impacted by tide cracks. They demarcated the zone using orange flares, which assisted the arriving crew to assess wind strength and direction.

Before departing Australia, the Soviets had proposed collecting me from Mawson during a routine flight between Molodezhnaya and Mirny. However, my arrival at Mawson left limited time before our scheduled departure for Dome C, so the only practical solution was a dedicated return flight from Mirny. Before arriving at Mawson, the Ilyushin 14 (IL14)[3] stopped at the Soviet's Soyuz field camp on the shores of Beaver Lake (now the site of a permanent Russian station known as Progress) to check on Soviet geologists prospecting in the Prince Charles Mountains. I wasn't totally special, as I had believed at the time, but this was my greatest-ever celebrity experience.

Friday 16 December 1983:

The aircraft arrived on schedule at 8:30am. I was the first to spot it emerging on the eastern horizon.

The IL14 made a thunderous noise on approach. It buzzed directly over us on the first pass, followed by a hard bank to the right in a

---

3. The IL14 was developed as a replacement for the Lisunov Li-2, a Soviet-built version of the American Douglas DC-3. The IL14 was intended for civil and military operations and was constructed in numerous configurations for both passenger and freight movements.

deafening roar as it headed out to loop around surrounding islands. We shrugged off the spine-tingling effects of this moment and speculated about their intentions: 'They're probably checking out the sea ice and wind strength … yes, yes, or maybe they're sight-seeing?' A fuzzy blowfly shape soon re-emerged downwind, flying slowly and gradually dropping altitude, obviously committed to a final approach. The IL14 dropped flaps about a kilometre out and zoomed in for a perfect three-point touchdown, skidding across the ice in front of us, then taxiing closer.

A six-hour flight from Mirny with no fuss, no landing aids, no fancy equipment, no beacons, and no radar – not even a graded ski way – just a welcoming group of Aussies standing on the ice in the middle of Kista Strait, waving like shipwrecked sailors. The Aeroflot livery shocked me into realising: this whole thing was really happening! The crew comprised a pilot (wearing a World War 2–like leather cap), co-pilot, radio operator, navigator, engineer and two passengers: Serdyukov, the station leader at Mirny, and Vlad, the leader of the Dome C traverse.

I was on the verge of tears, partly from emotion and anxiety about my inadequate language skills, but mainly due to intense headache and pain from the wound on my head. I worried about how to explain my black eye. Too late – the moment had arrived. I was the centre of attention. Accordingly I adopted rock-star style: a beanie and dark sunglasses which I wore at all times, even indoors, to minimise inconvenient questions. The Soviet guys later said they thought my injury was hilarious. It gave them plenty of material for gossip and bizarre rumours.

The arrival of the IL14 was a quasi-UFO experience. We had no prior information about an order of events or timings. The aircraft touched down and came to a halt. In the next surprising move, the commander shut down all engines. I had assumed the engines would remain running while my gear was quickly loaded. I imagined, obviously incorrectly, that I'd jump onboard and take off immediately. But no. Once the propellers were stationary, the rear door opened. A step ladder emerged. This was the UFO moment. We watched in awe – me, dressed in my best light blue overalls and, of course, my dark sunglasses and beanie, and the unidentified occupants silhouetted in black. They emerged one at a time, descending the ladder slowly with their backs to us, billowing steamy breath like dragons.

The first visitor approached. No-one knew who was who. The first minutes were awkward but everyone smiled. I felt butterflies in my stomach. I hoped, vainly, that no-one would expect me to say anything in Russian. Had we known they wanted to stay, we could have displayed names on sticky labels, but no-one thought they'd be hanging around for long. They couldn't understand us and we couldn't understand them. Jumbled, incoherent half-baked utterances bore faint resemblance to verbal communication. Fortunately, words didn't matter – the meaning was obvious from body language – vigorous handshakes and back slapping, accompanied by nodding heads and hugs, outstretched arms and pointing fingers (hey – look over there!), big smiles, shoulder shrugs and so on.

The only English speaker – Vladimir – was one of the last to emerge. Poised at the top of the ladder like a circus performer, he swung round and twisted to face us, hollering in English, 'Hello and welcome. It's great to be here,' or words to that effect. Vlad climbed down the ladder and stepped onto the ice with the moon-landing panache of Neil Armstrong. Herding the Soviet team to a nearby group of Mawsonites, he promptly introduced Station Leader Serdyukov, followed by each of the crew. By this stage, like penguins, all the stragglers had moved into our huddle.

Vlad's English was clear and accomplished. Phew! He spoke confidently with a whimsical lilt and occasional mispronunciation. Other Soviet crew members uttered the odd word or greeting in

English, mostly rehearsed phrases from school days. I was completely out of my depth. I avoided eye contact in case someone spoke to me in Russian and expected an answer. Fortunately, we had no agenda, no timetable and no speeches to deliver. Our visitors were in no obvious hurry to leave. Next, Vlad really surprised us. He requested an opportunity to travel to the station to meet Mawson scientists and inspect the magnetometer. With no inkling of this beforehand, I explained that the magnetometer that previously operated at Mawson was decommissioned years ago and no longer existed, which didn't seem to matter. 'Oh.' Vlad then asked, 'Could our team take station tour before return trip (sic)? We are not in hurry to leave. Also … weather forecast excellent!'

Their relaxed manner was refreshing but oddly unsettling. Our OIC seemed preoccupied by what he assumed was their inevitable need to top-up fuel. Perhaps he had read old diaries and knew of an incident in 1960 when the Russians dropped in for an unannounced refuelling stop on a flight between the Lazarev Ice Shelf and Mirny. Either way, after a flurry of discussion using hand gestures, our OIC was reassured. The Soviets definitely did not require fuel. But we also needed to load the plane. My gear filled the tray of a one tonne utility truck and took time to arrange. It included winter clothing, gifts packed in soft kitbags, numerous containers of equipment and a huge load of 'supplies' packaged in travel cases, crates and cardboard boxes. Once onboard I found it stacked mostly at the rear of the fuselage adjacent to a 200-litre drum of emergency diesel, loosely secured by slack rope.

Whereas the original American DC-3 was a tail dragger, the Soviet-built IL14 polar derivative had a nose-wheel with skis, and skis under the wheels that retracted into the wings. Instead of a standard 24-seat interior, this variant featured two long-range cylindrical fuel tanks inside the fuselage, each located on either side of the passenger aisle. Six passenger seats filled the remaining space. With its extra tanks, the IL14 could fly an impressive 3,000 km (from Mirny to Vostok and return, or a little under one-third the distance from the equator to the South Pole) without landing. Two IL14s based at Mirny provided air support to Vostok and shuttled personnel to and from Molodezhnaya during the summer at a frequency of two to three times per month.

Based on the advice of previous participants, I assembled provisions from Mawson to distribute at Mirny, partly for the wintering crew and partly for our traverse team. I collected multiple cartons of beer, wine, spirits, magazines, tinned and fresh foods, boxes of meat pies and a huge collection of condiments – Vegemite, peanut butter, jams and spicy sauces – plus souvenirs including lapel badges, stamps, flags, maps and novels. While the aircraft loaded, unoccupied crew members were invited, or goaded, into joyrides in the Odyssey go-carts, while Mawsonites cheered and watched. When finally packed, we jumped into the vehicles then headed to Mawson while the plane remained parked in Kista Strait. Serdyukov rode with the hoi polloi in a beach buggy. Others jumped into any vehicle with a spare seat. We communicated with sign language, mostly by finger pointing, interspersed with bouts of laughter.

Arrival at the station precipitated a rush to the bathroom, followed by the Soviet custom of sharing bread and salt – a symbol of prosperity and health and a signal that friendship has formed. The OIC and I launched into an impromptu station tour while Vlad headed off with the upper atmosphere science crew to inspect Mawson's science facilities. Our tour stopped at various vantage points for photo opportunities and views. I carried my pocket-size Russian–English dictionary and thumbed it desperately as we walked, searching for words, any words other than 'hello/privet'. The hectic activity and my throbbing head left me bereft of vocabulary. However, I do remember one sweet moment of communication success. We were walking down a hill between huts. Most of the

Soviet delegation were striding ahead, heading for the huskies, in which they had expressed interest. Our visitors didn't realise they needed to turn left. I called out loudly with my best Australian accent 'Na … leva' (which means 'to the left' in Russian) and the whole crew turned left, on cue. Wow, did I feel proud of myself! They had understood what I said! But, more importantly, I had also understood what I had said.

Mawson was, at the time, one of the last stations to retain working dog teams, a morale-boosting attraction for wintering expeditioners, but an anachronism elsewhere in Antarctica. The Soviets asked many questions, mostly by grunting and holding up fingers. They mingled cautiously with the dogs and enjoyed cuddling the litter of new puppies. We walked around pointing at objects and blurting compliments. Serdyukov revealed that Mirny's pet husky had recently died, then seized the moment to ask whether Mawson might have a puppy he could take back to Mirny. The OIC and Dale (the cook and dog handler) went off to discuss options. Rather than a puppy, Dale offered them a young dog called Snoopy, who was felt to have a more suitable temperament for life as a pet.[4]

The doctor was summoned and Snoopy sedated. During the final minutes of the visit, several Soviet guests visited the Mawson radio shack for a hurried session of philatelic swapping. Meanwhile, other Mawsonites collected a range of well-thumbed 'picture magazines' for circulation at Mirny.

---

4. In 1992 and 1993, huskies were withdrawn at the behest of the 1991 Madrid Protocol on Environmental Protection. The Protocol banned all introduced species except humans and required the removal of dogs from all Antarctic stations by 1994.

CHAPTER 3

First Encounters

YIKLA YOOAD

This is the life! Vostok, the Soviet Union's station high on the plateau of inland Antarctica.

Flight to Mirny

Friday 16 December 1983 continued:

Time to leave. Most of the station travelled out to the sea ice to witness our departure, a highly unusual and significant event. I felt like an astronaut being marched to the launch pad. I shook hands with colleagues, boarded the plane and was shown to a seat.

Prior to take-off, the chief pilot strolled down from the cockpit to the rear of the fuselage to inspect loading and adjust the centre of gravity. He pushed my bags around and juggled the position of the (full) 200-litre fuel drum. He rapped on the side of the long-range fuel tanks on his way back to test fluid levels. Slightly puzzled and seemingly unconvinced, he then shuffled off to the cockpit and returned with a flashlight and removed the filling caps to peer inside. The purpose was obvious, but struck me as rather unusual, and well.... wholly imprecise. I'm not sure what he expected to see. But it didn't faze the pilots, so it didn't faze me.

With the pre-flight checks complete, the plane revved up and taxied away. Inside, the noise was ear-shattering. The crew wore earphones but the unfortunate passengers had zero hearing protection. After lift-off, we banked steeply for a final fly past. I gazed out of a window to a sea of waving arms as we buzzed the group standing on the sea ice below. The pilot waved the wings then gained height. My thoughts bounced around trying to absorb every detail. I slumped into my seat obsessed by one thought: *This must be how astronauts feel when they blast off into space.*

Perfect weather provided smooth flying conditions and wonderful views. We avoided flying over water and generally followed the coastline to our left for most of the journey. At times the flight path took us further inland over the ice cap, but always within sight of the coast. The navigator checked compass headings routinely using an astrocompass mounted inside a Perspex observation dome in the roof of the fuselage. The navigator performed calculations by slide rule. The radio operator, who sat across the aisle from the navigator, communicated intermittently with both Mirny and Molodezhnaya using morse code. Activity inside the aircraft was mesmerising, so different from any previous aviation experience in my life to date. There were no business class seats on this flight, and definitely no drinks or meal service!

The captain invited me to the co-pilot seat during a particularly scenic section as we overflew Davis. He dialled up the emergency channel and contacted the Davis radio room, allowing me a brief opportunity to speak to Australian expeditioners. We couldn't chat for long as helicopters were involved in flying operations from *Nella Dan* somewhere below. I explained the purpose of my program, the places to which I was headed, and details of what I could see from the cockpit. The amazing panorama included, to our left, sea ice and icebergs dotting the horizon, enveloped in deep, hazy shades of blue, grey and white. To our right, views of the Vestfold Hills, sprouting like mushrooms from an endless white surface thousands of feet below. The crew brought Snoopy to the cockpit for a look around once the pre-flight sedation had worn off.

The scenery became more picturesque as we descended into Mirny. Closer to the ground the detail was clear and obvious, the subtle colours more distinct. Huge icebergs remained visible far out to sea. Vast stretches of confetti-like sea ice floated in the deep colours of coastal ocean set against a stunning foreground of ice cliffs and enormous penguin colonies. We banked to the right on the final approach where I caught my first glimpse of the station through the cockpit window. The main Mirny buildings were perched on a high rocky outcrop surrounded by numerous huts and a sprawling grave-yard of retired equipment.

The six-hour flight was noisy and tiring, but exhilarating. All hands pitched in to unload. Several of us jumped into a vehicle and headed to the station while the crew refuelled and secured air-craft tie-downs. The IL14 remained parked on the ski way, quite a distance from the station and not hangered. I was told, 'The com-pacted ski way was maintained by occasional grading and rolled with a steel drum. Snow density gauged visually' (sic). On arrival at the station proper, Slava, the doctor, escorted me to the surgery where I remained under observation for an hour or two. Next, I was transferred to a temporary room in Dom* Radio. My equipment was offloaded to the Kharkovchanka* apart from my personal bags, which stayed with me.

Dinner in the mess consisted of spaghetti in a watery sauce. After dinner, Vlad guided me to the *balok* (the over-snow living van we would use on the traverse) for introductions and drinks with traverse colleagues – recently arrived from locations accurately described as 'around the globe', including Vostok, Molodezhnaya, Moscow and Melbourne.

Our team of nine consisted of:

- Vladimir Papitashvili (Vlad) – magnetologist, traverse leader, navigator and lead scientist. Vlad arrived at Mirny by air from Moscow in mid-November, accompanied by two technicians (the 'two Valentines'), all employed by Moscow's Institute for Terrestrial Magnetism.
- Valentine G – general technician. Valentine assisted Vlad with technical support including the installation, repair and maintenance of automatic remote magnetic stations (ARMS).
- Valentine K – electronics technician who also supported Vlad with similar responsibilities as Valentine G. Valentine was the only team member to have previously travelled the Mirny to Dome C route.
- Sergey – cook and/or magnetologist. Sergey assisted Vlad with scientific measurements and was the only non-smoker apart from me. He had spent the previous winter at Molodezhnaya.
- Vyacheslav (Slava) – doctor and abdominal surgeon. Slava had spent the previous winter at Vostok.
- Valery – chief mechanic and the driver of Kharkovchanka 2. This was his first time in Antarctica.
- Sergey – radio operator. Sergey had spent the bulk of his career working on fishing vessels.
- Sergey – mechanic. The youngest in our team at 24 years of age. Married with one daughter, Sergey was responsible for maintaining and driving the Artilleriskiy Tyagach Tyazholiy (ATT*) prime mover. This was also his first time in Antarctica.
- Treeva Kalinovitch Hamlikov – glaciologist, Australian, 29 years old. The ninth member of the team, who had previously wintered at Casey.

Russian male names include a patronymic based on the father's given name. Typically, Russians summon each other by a combination of either first name or first name and patronymic. In a similar vein to social convention in Australia, nicknames and terms of endearment apply between individuals based on familiarity and relationships. Russian males may summon each other by surname or a diminutive of the given name. Ultimately though, the individual will advise others on how they prefer to be addressed. Prior to leaving Mirny we discussed these conventions in friendly banter. I was anointed 'Treeva Kalinovitch (pronounced kalinitch) Hamlikov', the patronymic based on my father's given name, which also coincides with my actual middle name. An appropriate attribution, I was told. Kalinovitch sounded similar to the Russian word for 'red berry' – a jokey-reference to my (then) hair colour. Mostly however, I was simply called 'Tref' or 'Treeva'.

We toasted with half a glass shot from a container of 'double-strength vodka', supplemented by various brands of regular vodka and beer. My introduction to double-strength vodka was interesting. Whereas a seasoned Russki could easily gulp half a glass, I found one sniff enough to gag, but I had to give it a go to be sociable. 'Put aside half a glass of vodka as a chaser,' they said, adding, 'best have an open can of beer on standby, just in case,' wink, wink. During the evening we discussed family, childhood experiences, schools, global politics and current affairs. Vlad translated. The topic of Soviet soldiers killed in World War 2 was explained and reinforced many times during my visit to Mirny. The alcohol we consumed either assisted or impeded conversation – depending on how you looked at it. In 1983, Cold War tensions between the United States and the Soviet Union were at the highest level since the Cuban Missile crisis and the U-2 spy plane incident. The Korean Airline incident also raised its head immediately in our initial conversation – not surprising given the timing of my arrival.

Korean Air Lines Flight 007 (KAL007), a scheduled Boeing 747 flight from New York City to Seoul via Anchorage, Alaska was shot down by a Soviet Sukhoi Su-15 interceptor on 1 September

1983, three months before my arrival at Mirny. KAL007 drifted from its original planned route into prohibited Soviet air space and Soviet Air Forces treated the unidentified aircraft as an intruding US spy plane. They destroyed it with air-to-air missiles after allegedly firing warning shots which were likely not seen by the KAL pilots.

Twenty-three years earlier (on 1 May 1960), the Soviets shot down an actual US spy plane in controversial circumstances. The so-called U-2 incident doesn't excuse the hostility towards KAL007, but does demonstrate the political paranoia behind such actions. The Americans claimed initially that the US plane shot down in 1960 was a weather research aircraft that strayed off course (sounds familiar!). It was actually a CIA spy plane – a Lockheed U-2 thought to be beyond the reach of Soviet jets and missiles. The U-2 was hit by one of 14 Soviet S-75 Dvina surface-to-air missiles. Less well known is the fact that another of the S-75 missiles also hit a Soviet MiG jet fighter sent to intercept the U-2. The 30-year-old U-2 pilot Francis Gary Powers parachuted to safety inside Soviet territory and was captured immediately, along with parts of the airplane's surveillance equipment including photographs of Soviet military bases. The Soviet MiG pilot ejected but died from his injuries. The U-2 incident seriously set back summit talks underway in Paris at the time between Khrushchev and Eisenhower.

Fast forward now to Malaysia Airlines Flight 17 (MH17) – a scheduled passenger flight from Amsterdam to Kuala Lumpur. MH17 was shot down by a Russian Buk surface-to-air missile on 17 July 2014 while flying over eastern Ukraine. All 283 passengers and 15 crew were killed. Wreckage from the Boeing 777 aircraft was found near Hrabove in Donetsk Oblast, Ukraine, 40 km from the Russian border. The reason for this attack remains unclear but seems likely to have been another case of mistaken identity, this time associated with hostilities between Russia and Ukraine.

Our party continued until 2am, by which time we were thoroughly good friends. My colleagues were clearly upset by the circumstances of KAL007, and the suffering and embarrassment inflicted on ordinary Soviet citizens by the unwelcome actions of authoritarian leadership. It was the era of Yuri Andropov's 15-month tenure as General Secretary of the Communist Party, an unprecedented period in Soviet history. Mikhail Gorbachev was the rising star, the youngest and one of the most active and visible members of the Politburo. Two years later, in 1985, Gorbachev took over as General Secretary and introduced Perestroika and Glasnost.

Initial Impressions

Saturday 17 December 1983:

Although now at Mirny, I remained unclear about the timing of our departure for Dome C. I promptly raised the subject, with both Vlad and the station OIC, of a possible visit to Vostok to remeasure the ice movement station established 6 or 7 years earlier and not yet re-measured. Obtaining a surface velocity data point at Vostok was critical to our glaciology objectives. Vlad and the OIC agreed immediately. It seemed we would leave for Dome C after visiting Vostok. A new engine was being fitted to the ATT and the prime movers were not quite ready.

The following morning, I woke at 7am to an ear-shattering, cymbal-crashing, offensively loud blast through the public address system 'DAAAAAAAAAAAAA!!! … Keeeerrrash!!!!' It was the attention-grabbing opening note to the State Anthem of the Soviet Union! So strong were the emotions it caused, my eyes burst open despite a groggy hangover. I felt compelled to sit upright and salute. Little wonder it is widely regarded as the most stirring national anthem of all time. Breakfast in the mess commenced at 8am. When I didn't show up on time, Poshar (a cook) kindly came and knocked on my door. None of my traverse colleagues had stirred. I went over to the balok after breakfast and set up the JMR for practice and charged the batteries. Vlad and I discussed the science program and objectives. I showed him my priority list of ice-movement remeasurement stations.

On my second night at Mirny, oceanographer Oleg (also a fluent English speaker) invited Vlad and me to join him for a 'tea party'. Oleg wintered the previous year at Mirny, collecting snow samples from sites within 10 km of the station and analysing them for chemical impurities. We drank tea and conversed in English about everyday life, occasionally discussing work matters. During the early days with the Soviets, I felt relatively isolated. Some expeditioners seemed more curious than serious about engaging me in conversation. Most early exchanges were a test of their high school English, usually finishing with spinning eyeballs and puzzled looks on both sides. I often found myself thinking *what aaaaare you saying?*, although I am first to admit my appalling Russian must have been very confusing to them. Some of my hosts avoided eye contact altogether. I assume they felt conversation with me required more effort than it was worth.

By the time we returned from traverse, this attitude had changed significantly. Having been immersed in conversational Russian and learning new words every day for several months, I could by then participate in slow conversation – providing my companions kept the language simple. I could communicate, but most importantly, I was well rehearsed at swearing. My accent prompted regular taunts. 'Ha, say that again … the phrase about mothers.' My hosts were often in stitches of laughter depending on the amount of theatre I invoked.

Numerous expeditioners enquired about my government 'reporting' obligations. The questions seemed unnervingly earnest and more than naïve curiosity. I laughed things off initially, trying to not appear shocked. But I was shocked! My mumbled denials probably caused the opposite effect. The experience reminded me of a 'joke'.

During a break in a summit meeting in Moscow, President Eisenhower asked Nikita Khrushchev whether he collected stories against himself.

'Yes I do,' replied Khrushchev.

'Do you have many?' asked Eisenhower.

'Two prisons full,' said Khrushchev.

Within the Soviet population, funny stories and jokes about the political regime and public lives disguised fears about overstepping the official order where even that which is not forbidden is not necessarily permitted. At Mirny, several expeditioners suggested two KGB agents were among the station cohort, an open secret blurted to me with the zeal of religious confession. I was, however, already familiar with Soviet security, having travelled across Russia on the Trans-Siberian Railway as a student.

The Mirny wintering team included an official artist, a bizarre appointment from my perspective, but understandable for this society. It seemed to be a hybrid role of graffiti artist and signwriter. The artist prepared politically inspired murals, as well as signs and placards for May Day celebrations and 'demonstrations' – a solemn and serious parade occasion, the cultural equivalent to our ANZAC Day.

First impressions of Mirny were lacklustre. Austere living quarters and a barren mess area augmented poor sanitation and sour bathroom odours that permeated building corridors. The buildings were neither exclusively residential nor exclusively workplace. Most expeditioners lived and worked within the same building. Most, but not all, shared a room. Bedrooms featured pressed metal walls and ceilings with vinyl floor coverings and no carpet. Some residents hung blankets and woven carpets on the wall, for both decoration and insulation. An internal telephone and public address system connected all rooms. Hot water column heaters maintained the indoor temperature via a centralised supply from the powerhouse. Small exterior windows provided light, but no opportunity for views.

Soviet Antarctic expeditions did not recruit women, a strange contradiction I thought, given the integration between men and women in the conventional Soviet workplace. In those years, females at Soviet Antarctic stations seemed to be regarded as either a distraction or inconvenience. After meals and particularly after the evening dinner, men played dice games and chess while squatting in corridors near the mess. They smoked heavily, conversed garrulously and generally passed the time before returning to their sleeping quarters. Clouds of cigarette smoke choked the corridors constantly during the evening. Dedicated recreation areas were virtually non-existent, other than one cold, stark library and one pool table in the mess. We did not have a gym or lounge area. The pool table was popular and always surrounded by players, who gathered around it after meals. Singing was a manly thing. Occasionally a guitar, balalaika or even a piano accordion would appear from nowhere and a group would start singing.

Mirny swarmed with personnel and choked from accommodation shortages over the summer. During my visit, numbers swelled from a typical wintering population of around 60, to 140. Transient personnel such as builders travelling to and from Vostok, and personnel shuttling to and from Molodezhnaya, exacerbated the numbers of outgoing and incoming wintering crew. During summer, expeditioners shared rooms and many other available spaces. Some lived and slept in over-snow traverse vehicles. Others set up makeshift sleeping and eating arrangements in their office or workplace.

Half of the wintering crew were scientists or technicians, the other half tradespeople and support staff, admin, doctors and aviation crew. The 1983 wintering team included seven geophysicists. The meteorological office employed two people, and the aerology section employed two more to track balloon flights and measure wind speed, temperature and pressure. A biology research program was not current at the time. Meteorological observers conducted bird observations on a voluntary basis. Three cooks staffed the kitchen, assisted by a nominated slushy* rostered from the remainder of the men. At mealtimes, the cooks plated food in the kitchen then passed meals through a servery in the wall to a waiting queue of men in the mess. Cafeteria-style seating accommodated 6 to 8 men per table. You could sit anywhere. On the way out, diners scraped leftovers into a slops bucket, then dropped dirty dishes into a rinsing bucket for slushies to wash by hand. Automatic dishwashers and clothes washing machines were not available at Mirny, or if they were I didn't know their whereabouts. The dining room décor featured a supersized chessboard attached to the wall. Pieces from both teams hung from hooks on the wall, to show the state of play. A group at Mirny played regular games against a group in Moscow, the moves exchanged daily by radio.

Beyond the perimeter of the main buildings, a potential death-trap of slots and cracks in the ice (crevasses) discouraged residents from unsupervised meandering. 'For safety reasons pedestrians must stay within established tracks marked by poles and connecting rope lines,' station leadership warned. The main accommodation/work building, Dom Radio, was situated on a rock outcrop at the highest point of the site.

Sunday 18 December 1983:

I woke at 4am to the growing sound of an incoming blizzard. The building shook as if affected by earthquake. My thoughts turned immediately to the JMR antenna l had erected on the roof of the balok. I couldn't see the balok from my room and I panicked. I dressed hurriedly and jogged outside. Fortunately, the antenna was intact so I dismantled it immediately, took a few photos and returned to bed. The blizzard would obviously delay our flight to Vostok.

The wind blew relentlessly for the remainder of the morning, giving me a chance to re-organise my bag for the Vostok visit. Suddenly, mid-afternoon, the wind ceased. Serdyukov, the officer in charge of the station, invited a small group including me to his quarters for yet-another welcoming party. His beverage of choice was Ararat brandy, a cognac-style spirit from Armenia, arguably the premier drink in the USSR and, according to Serdyukov, the favourite cognac of Winston Churchill. Normally not a spirit drinker, I did enjoy this one. Strong coffee and exquisite chocolates were served as the conversation meandered across topics including the possibilities for an ongoing USSR/Australia exchange program, and the current state of the Australian Antarctic building program. I presented Serdyukov with a Tasmanian wilderness calendar, a bottle of Ballantine's whisky and a carton of Benson & Hedges cigarettes. We talked until well after midnight.

That same evening an unexpected telex arrived for me from Davis, printed in Cyrillic characters. After puzzling for a long period, I realised the message required a reader to sound the Cyrillic letters phonetically to reconstitute English words (the Russian radio operators could only transmit Cyrillic characters). It wasn't easy or obvious to do this. I wrestled with the meaning for two or three days and some words still remain indecipherable today. The tongue-in-cheek message originated from a glaciology colleague and read, as best I could make out:

> *Dear Comrade Trevor of the Antarctic, hope your work is getting along well, and that all the Western technology instruments the JMR satellite receiver are still working just fine. If you get lost just remember your results since one pass measured is still around +/– 10 m. Anyway, hope you are holding together also, have a Merry Christmas. Cheerio.*

The Coldest Place on Earth

Monday 19 December 1983:

Breakfast at 2am preceded departure for Vostok at 4am. I only had two hours sleep!

Visiting Vostok was arguably the most exhilarating and one of the most sickening experiences of my life. Vlad accompanied me as translator and technical assistant. Slava, now officially the appointed traverse team doctor, was concerned about my ability to cope with altitude given my head wound. He therefore came along to monitor my health and wellbeing.

The outbound flight took five hours to travel the 1,420 km straight line distance to Vostok, at an average speed over ground of 280 km/hr, or 150 knots. For most of the journey we crabbed along at 70 m above the surface, bashing into strong headwinds and whiteout, straining to navigate by following the surface tracks of overland tractor trains. Vostok (78°S, 107°E) lies a little to the east of due south (true) from Mirny. If you were to continue travelling due south over a similar distance, you would eventually arrive at the South Geographic Pole.

Operating the IL14 close to the surface was stressful and intensely manual for the entire crew, not just the pilots. Several times the surface tracks disappeared, forcing the co-pilot to focus on scanning for tracks while the pilot in command maintained control over altitude and direction. At various times we dropped down and almost skimmed the surface in our search for the elusive tracks by which we were navigating. To alleviate cockpit workload, the flight engineer handled trim adjustments while kneeling between the pilot and co-pilot! Back to base communications were issued and received by morse code, just as they were during the flight from Mawson. The astrocompass was almost useless due to constant whiteout.

I became increasingly nauseous as the aircraft gained height. I tried to deal with it by leaning forward and placing my head between my hands. The experience was worse than the worst form of seasickness. I felt like vomiting the entire time. I couldn't lie in the aircraft aisle, so I lay on top of the fuel tanks where I remained for most of the flight, returning to my seat just prior to landing. My legs felt like jelly on arrival. Unable to support myself, Vlad and Slava carried me down the ladder and assisted me across the ski way to the nearest building.

My hosts directed me to the OIC's living quarters where I rested while the Vostok crew moved a hut to a temporary position five metres from the marker pole I'd come to remeasure. By afternoon, I'd managed to get myself together and set up the JMR but I felt like vomiting the entire time. I started the machine and returned to bed, unable to concentrate or think clearly. Vlad offered invaluable assistance. He checked the JMR at 8pm while I remained immobilised by headache and dizziness. Several times through the night, Slava and Vlad visited to check on my condition.

They had good reason to be concerned. At an elevation of 3,489 m above sea level, Vostok is equivalent in elevation to Cusco (3,400 m), the historic capital of the Inca empire in the Andes, Peru. It is 60% higher than Mt Kosciuszko (2,228 m) Australia's tallest mountain, and comparable in elevation to Antarctica's Mt Erebus (3,794 m). Altitude sickness affects individuals differently, but at elevations above 2,500 m it wreaks havoc for those vulnerable. I hadn't flown to high altitude before, let alone in the Antarctic.

Vostok, which means 'east' in Russian, earned its title as the coldest place on Earth in July 1983, 5 months before my visit, by recording an official world record minimum temperature of -89.2°C – a standing record today. Vostok 'polyarniks'* (Soviet polar workers) who lived through the cold snap explained matter-of-factly how the official minimum measured in a Stevenson screen[5] two metres above

5. An instrument shelter designed by Scottish civil engineer Thomas Stevenson to provide a standard environment to measure temperature, humidity, dewpoint and atmospheric pressure.

the surface was exceeded by an unofficial minimum of -90°C measured at the snow surface. Vostok's unique location in the centre of Antarctica was acknowledged by the Americans who, in 1980, constructed two enormous radio masts to facilitate communications between Vostok, McMurdo and the South Pole, a wonderful symbol of apolitical cooperation encouraged by the *Antarctic Treaty*. During that same year, an American physicist also wintered at Vostok, continuing a long tradition where one American scientist was invited to winter at a Soviet station and one Soviet, in turn, was invited to winter at a US station. His hut, still in use for geophysics and ionospheric studies, was offered to me during my short stay.

Vostok was established as a scientific research station during the International Geophysical Year in 1957/58. It is remote, high and sits over some of the thickest ice (between three and four kilometres thick) in Antarctica. The location is ideally suited to the study of glaciology, magnetology and climatology. Ice drilling commenced at Vostok in 1958, using thermal drills manufactured onsite from makeshift materials and equipment. The first deep drilling attempt began in April 1970. Two decades of persistent endeavour yielded five separate boreholes, with the drilling program attracting worldwide interest. The deep core drilling was in partnership with the Laboratoire de Glaciologie et Geophysique de l'Environment (LGGE) in Grenoble, France.

During the 1970s, glaciologists calculated that Vostok overlay a region of the continent with liquid water at the base of the ice mass. The prediction was theoretical, based on mathematical models showing temperatures at the base of the ice sheet to be in the pressure-melting range of -5°C to -10°C. Radar altimeter data confirmed the theory in the 1990s by delineating a 20 km–long flat spot in the surface topography, in contrast to the surrounding rough topography. Vostok station is now known to directly overlie a position at the southern end of the vast subglacial Lake Vostok.

International interest in Soviet ice core drilling turned to concern when Soviet scientists announced plans to sample the underlying water. What started in 1958 as ice drilling to acquire englacial data (such as temperature distribution, biochemical and chemical analysis) for the study of ice sheet physics and climate history, morphed into a program to study the properties of the subglacial water itself. They hoped to discover unique life forms and learn something about the evolution of life in the distant past. In 2006, the borehole reached a depth of 3,650 m, less than 100 m above the subglacial lake. Drilling halted temporarily while Soviet scientists determined what they considered to be an environmentally responsible plan for final penetration.

Tuesday 20 December 1983:

At 7am, although drenched by cold sweat and suffering intense headache and dizziness, I managed to trudge unassisted to the ice movement measurement pole. The JMR had ceased functioning overnight. The battery voltage display indicated seven volts – way too low.

Despite the premature and unexpected equipment failure I had collected 21 satellite passes from a possible maximum of 28. More than enough for an accurate position fix. The JMR-004 became unserviceable at its first assignment. My woeful physical state prevented me forming immediate ideas about the cause of the failure. I continued to think about it for weeks afterwards, trying to decide whether it was operational error on my part, or just bad luck. Thankfully, the second unit, JMR-1, at Mirny was available for the remainder of the expedition.

I returned to my bunk and didn't eat until dinner time. OIC Budretsky invited Vlad, Slava, the chief mechanic and me to pre-dinner drinks in his office. We toasted with the now familiar Ararat brandy. Accompaniments included red and black caviar on bread (big grey caviar the size of ball bearings), ekra (pureed zucchini), salami, preserved fish, ham, eggplant dip and herrings. A relentless headache and nausea suppressed my appetite. I found it difficult to face alcoholic drinks. Instead, I reached for pineapple-flavoured chocolates and shortbreads. The sweets agreed more with my fragile stomach than the alternative of eggplant dip and pickled herrings.

We discussed a now familiar range of topics, including station life at Vostok and daily routines. OIC Budretsky explained how difficult men found physical work at Vostok, especially if outside for more than one hour. 'Exhaled breath causes your eyelids to freeze together,' he said. *Something to remember for next time* I thought. Apart from the obvious limitations of cold and altitude, one glance at the scattered arrangement of buildings confirmed the obvious constraints on leisure activities. Popular pastimes included movies, reading and chess. The OIC chatted about the procedures to prepare a cup of hot tea. An odd topic, maybe, but interesting given that the low ambient air pressure allows water to boil at a temperature 25% lower than at sea level. At Vostok, a finger plunged into boiling water will not burn. It feels like the temperature of a hot shower. To increase the boiling point, you must increase pressure, typically by fitting a tight lid to the kettle or saucepan, then filling it completely (no air gap if possible) before applying heat. The low air pressure also caused bottled carbonated water to spew its contents in a foamy explosion of bubbles when the cap was released, unless you took preventative action. To avoid losing half the contents, the method involved placing a drinking vessel over the opening as the top was removed, then carefully but quickly inverting the bottle and cup as the contents spewed out.

Human adaptation to Vostok altitude typically requires three months, at least that was their rule of thumb. Altitude seems to affect different people in different ways. I noticed several Vostok expeditioners were hyperventilating, including the OIC. I seemed to be the only incoming visitor immediately and visibly affected to the extent of nausea, headaches and insomnia. Humidity was non-existent. My mouth, nose and throat felt dry the entire time. We chatted at length about how to cope with 'extreme cold'. Apparently, every one of the 21 Vostok winterers undertook their normal routines (including daily outdoor activity) through the bone-chilling cold-snap the previous July.

After returning from the Dome C traverse months later, I learned more about Vostok from a weather observer who also lived through the July '83 winter. He told me, 'For nine days straight – from 7 July to 15 July 1983 – the outside air temperature remained below -75°C, followed by one full week from 15 July to 21 July, during which the temperature always remained below –80°C.' Imagine living through three continuous weeks of darkness during which the air temperature never warmed higher than -75°C. During summer, Vostok temperatures typically vary between -22°C and -40°C. The maximum recorded temperature at Vostok is -14°C. So, when I read my diary entry noting, 'The temperature today is -25°C, in contrast to yesterday's -37°C,' I realised I had possibly experienced a Vostok heatwave on my second day!

While extreme cold and geographic isolation impose tough psychological and physical constraints, they don't necessarily mean a high fatality risk. However, Vostok has had its share of fatal accidents. On 12 April 1982, a fire erupted in the power station and claimed the life of the chief mechanic. This fire was outside the season where personnel could be evacuated by air or over-snow traverse. A tractor train from Mirny, for instance, would have taken 6 weeks to reach Vostok had it been able, and even if the weather were favourable, sufficient personnel would have been unavailable. Barely eight months later on 26 December 1982, a second fire destroyed the deep ice core drilling shelter. The second fire didn't result in loss of life, but it did halt the borehole drilling program midway through the third deep borehole attempt.

Antarctica is unforgiving when it comes to accidents. The clean-up from both Vostok fires continued during my visit in December 1983. Incredibly, the Vostok team of 1982 hunkered down after the power station fire to endure the brunt of winter, without proper power, heating or lights. They lived and worked in dispersed plywood and aluminium huts and maintained warmth by huddling around candlelike heating devices of wicks dipped in kerosene. The wicks, twisted partly out of asbestos fibre, produced clouds of soot from incomplete combustion in Vostok's rarefied atmosphere. Men's faces were temporarily blackened by carbon particles embedded in the skin for months afterwards. Somehow, the men rallied and repaired a previously scrapped diesel unit to restore partial power. Despite chronic hardship, they continued meteorological observations and a rudimentary science program. On return to the Soviet Union, members of the Vostok '82 expedition were awarded well-deserved medals.

Another unique consideration for Vostok winterers is the time commitment away from home – at least 18 months. Most of the men have little to no contact with their families during this time. The sea voyage from the Soviet Union to Antarctica takes six weeks. Add another six weeks to travel by tractor train to Vostok, then double it for the return journeys and add a 12-month term at the station and you have 18 months, sometimes more. Vostok polyarniks are partly motivated by money. They accrue higher allowances than person-nel at Mirny. Adventure is also a factor, just as it is for Australians. But for Australians who leave Australia and arrive in Antarctica in summer, the change in climate is immediate and dramatic. Soviet expeditioners depart during the northern hemisphere winter to arrive in Antarctica during the southern hemisphere summer. For many Russians, the wildlife may be different, or in the case of Vostok totally absent, but the climate is not so different. Nevertheless, numerous expeditioners winter at Vostok on multiple occasions.

The incumbent OIC had just finished his second term, the cook his third term. A mechanic was completing a seventh wintering term, a bewildering feat. Although not as common, some Vostok personnel stay for consecutive winters.

Vostok mean minimum temperatures hover around -65°C consistently for six months of the year, from April through to September. Over a similar period, the mean minimum temperature at coastal Antarctic stations typically ranges between -13°C to -21°C. At Mawson, for instance, the mean annual temperature is around -15°C. At Vostok, it is -53°C. For many Australians, extreme cold experiences involve a flirtation with alpine activities, or a commercial cold room or a refrigerated container. Most of us can feel or guess ambient temperature without looking at a thermometer – if the temperature is within a familiar range of say 10°C to 30°C. To imagine 'how it feels' in temperatures of -80°C is unfathomable, unless the experience occurs in gradual increments. The difference between an air temperature of -20°C and -40°C is just as significant as the difference in feeling between 0°C and -20°C. Similarly, the difference between -40°C and -60°C is just as significant as the difference between -20°C to -40°C. Scandinavians have a saying, 'There's no such thing as bad weather, only bad clothing.'

Dressing for the Antarctic is about layering and wearing clean woollen layers underneath windproof outer garments. During a blizzard, irrespective of the external temperature, the priority is to repel the devilish effects of wind by closing every opening and covering every part of the body, especially the head and neck. High-tech materials are not necessary. A key factor to maintaining warmth is clean garments, particularly socks and underclothing.

At temperatures below -20°C, exhaled breath condenses and re-freezes noticeably on facial hair and clothing around the mouth and cheeks. At temperatures below -30°C it is vitally important to scan each other's exposed extremities regularly for indications of frostbite, signified by white patches to the cheeks, nose or fingers. At -60°C, the average expeditioner is probably wearing three times the number of layers and three times the thickness of clothing a person requires at 0°C. Frostbite is a burn and, just like sunburn, the individual may not notice it initially. A white patch must be addressed immediately. On most occasions, the effect of low-level frostbite is minimised by cupping hands over the affected region and exhaling warm air. But, if the white patch is large, an affected person must retreat indoors and warm up thoroughly.

At Vostok, personnel scuffed around in thick felt boots called 'vallinke'*, a boot with no sole or tread. The powdery soft and smooth surface reduced the need for the normal arch support provided by a stiff sole. Wearing vallinke involved a process of wrapping your foot in cloth strips – like bandages, then covering the strips with a thin sock to hold them in place before inserting your foot into the boot. I experimented with vallinke at Vostok but couldn't get comfortable. I did not like the lack of a sole or the lack of traction. My feet did not feel warm and I didn't try them again until after we reached Dome C, weeks later.

Apart from the cold temperatures, another annoying and unexpected aspect of Antarctic weather is static electricity generated during blizzards. Just as you can be zapped by a metal door handle after scuffing your shoes on the carpet in a car, the same occurs in Antarctica if you touch a metal door handle with bare hands (or lightly gloved hands) during a blizzard. After several zaps, you quickly learn to discharge static by brushing door handles with the back of your hand before grabbing the handle fully.

Wednesday 21 December 1983:

My last day at Vostok. Vlad gave me a call at 7am. Slava joined us for breakfast. Feeling slightly better, I devoured two bowls of porridge plus a cup of tea. Our returning aircraft was due at 9:30am, giving us one hour for sightseeing.

By this stage I could walk unassisted although my head throbbed. Vlad and I headed to the drilling shed to inspect the ice core thermal drill, attended by technicians from the Mining Institute of (then) Leningrad. The chief driller 'explained me' (sic) the operating method – in Russian. I struggled to follow, pleading for him to slow down. Vlad filled in the gaps by translating. Much of what I learned was inferred from body language. I understood sporadic parts of the verbal explanation, occasionally noting an interesting fact or figure. Apparently, the current borehole commenced after fire destroyed the rig in 1982. At that time, the drillers had penetrated two kilometres below the surface, approximately halfway to bedrock. During my visit the new borehole depth was 300 m. Drilling operations involved two men working 10-hour shifts, from 8am to 6pm every day. A third team member worked on the clean-up of fire debris at the old site. They didn't run a night shift. The drilling shed measured 18 m x 3.5 m – the size of a large shipping container, with a 15 m high tower attached. Deep borehole drilling occurred in three stages. Stage 1 was a dry hole constructed using a thermal melt head to a depth of one kilometre. Stage 2 was a liquid-filled hole from a depth between one and two kilometres. Stage 3 employed a 'special' melt head with a transformer to convert high voltage AC power to a lower voltage for working purposes.

Vlad and I ambled around the station, taking in views from various angles. We paused to pay our respects at the small monument of the deceased mechanic from the 1982 fire. Slava joined us just before reboarding. I enjoyed the return air journey far more than the outbound leg. Superb weather and superb visibility. The lower we dropped, the better I felt. We landed at Komsomolskaya to refuel and stretch, another unexpected bonus. We had 30 minutes to look around – more than enough given the lack of physical structures. Komsomolskaya is 760 km inland of Mirny, about halfway to Vostok, and is actually 200 m higher than Vostok. Established in 1957 as a permanent station, Komsomolskaya now functions as a seasonal outpost and fuel-dump to support tractor trains travelling between Mirny and Vostok.

Again, I was invited to the co-pilot's seat, where the aircrew cross-examined me with questions about family and life in Australia. I had a turn at the controls. It felt like three seconds, but may have been closer to a minute or two. I passed around a selection of wedding photos featuring my beautiful 25-year-old wife, which generated a flood of flirtatious remarks. The crew stared goggle-eyed at Kerry's photo, passing it backwards and forwards between themselves. Shortly before arrival at Mirny, we flew over the traverse party heading for Dome B. Naturally, we swooped. The pilot waved the wings as we circled before landing at 4pm. Enough time remained to stow bags and race to the banya* (Russian sauna/bathhouse). I was so relieved to be back at sea level.

Evening dinner consisted of fried pork fillet with cold beans and sauerkraut. The dessert of Russian 'kompot' featured a smoky brown, watery version of today's uber trendy stewed-fruit compote. Russian kompot wasn't my idea of dessert. As a 29-year-old I craved a huge bowl of bananas and ice-cream, something I wouldn't experience again until I returned to Australia. That evening I weighed myself – 69.6kg – or 3kg lighter than my father when he was released as a Prisoner of War from the Thai Burma Railway.

CHAPTER 4

The Traverse

YINYV YIZAB YONZZ YIMOR

I am leaving the station for a short while don't worry. I am setting out on a tractor traverse journey to Dome C Wilkes Land, a United States summer glaciology research station situated at 74° S, 124° E. Radio reception has been very bad.

Preparations

Mirny dispatched four inland expeditions during the 1983/84 summer – all of a similar distance to ours. Two were resupply traverses to Vostok, the third a science traverse to Dome B that departed Mirny one day ahead of ours, the same party we overflew on our return flight from Vostok.

The first Vostok resupply traverse that departed in November '83 returned to Mirny during the Christmas/New Year period, just after we left. A logistics behemoth, it delivered building materials and stores for the completion of the recently destroyed powerhouse. The 16 vehicles and 29 personnel (20 of whom were mechanics) spent two months completing the round trip. The second Vostok traverse of 14 men and 8 vehicles departed one week after the first resupply traverse returned and towed bulk diesel (only) to support Vostok winter operations.

I learned for the first time of my likely return to Australia aboard the passenger vessel *Baikal*, scheduled to arrive at Mirny in early to mid-April 1984. We needed to be back several weeks before *Baikal* arrived – in other words, by mid-March 1984. An undersupply of station accommodation was additional encouragement to get under-way immediately. In the space of a few days, we tied down equipment, loaded stores and fuel, assembled food rations and packed clothing. I, meanwhile, worked frantically to test run JMR-1.

Thursday 22 December 1983:

We departed Mirny at 4pm – exactly one week after I arrived.

We made an early pitstop on the station outskirts to withdraw rations from an ice cave where the station's bulk meats were stored. Vlad and Valery emerged with half-carcasses of beef and pork on each shoulder, whereafter we hoicked them onto the living van roof and jammed them into boxes alongside various crates of tools and equipment. The carcasses were not wrapped, and we didn't have a bandsaw. *How on earth can we butcher those things*, I wondered. I noticed we had an axe – a domestic axe, not an ice-axe – the sharp side was perfect for butchering, the blunt side surprisingly useful for grinding peppercorns and sometimes hammering track pins[*].

Two small flags adorned a flagpole attached to the Kharkovchanka. The highest was a small Russian flag, which flew above a souvenir-sized Australian flag that I brought with me. Serdyukov, along with station dignitaries, joined us for a send-off at a rallying point beyond the ice cave, near the airfield. Valery discharged flares while the rest of us exchanged handshakes accompanied by vigorous backslapping. That was that. Dome C here we come!

First Stop Pionerskaya

Slowly, slowly the coast disappeared, along with all colours beyond a vestige of grey, blue and various shades of white. The clear blue horizon visible at the coast dissolved into a hazy fuzz as grey skies merged with the whitish-grey of lightly blowing surface snow, disrupted only by occasional rock outcrops visible as muddy brown stains. Disappearing colours were matched proportionally by disappearing bird life and the total absence of other living organisms – apart from our own beating hearts and bacteria.

Day one was tough on the prime movers. They coughed, spluttered and gushed black smoke for most of the day. Vehicle crawler tracks lost grip on occasional steep sections, slipping sideways as the tractor train concertinaed, scaring the living daylights out of us. Our first day was one of the most gruelling and demanding of the entire journey. Progress slowed with frequent stops to experiment with gear changes and vehicle settings, and to tinker with tow arrangements or tighten load tie-downs and towing shackles. Our drivers gnashed and crunched gears to maintain momentum and assert control over recalcitrant sleds. Driving a tractor train involved a deft process of pulling levers, stamping pedals, flicking switches and dials and swivelling around regularly to check that nothing had fallen off or been left behind. Within hours of departure, an IL14 flew over the top in a spine-tingling moment of tradition and ritual. On hearing the familiar roar we pulled up and jumped down from the vehicles to wave and yell as the plane swooped on its way past. Cameras clicked furiously. Camaraderie was high.

Day 1 focussed on stress-testing machinery, rather than striving for distance. Declared a success (camped just 20 km from Mirny), we celebrated with pre-dinner toasts and impassioned speeches followed by lively singing after dinner. Moments after parking, I powered up the Astro C, hoping to contact Earl or any amateur in Melbourne who might contact Kerry. My first attempt was enthusiastic but a dismal failure. The radio hissed and spluttered and refused to transmit. Despite this hiccup I remained optimistic. I expected difficulties due to an effect called polar cap absorption (PCA)*. I continued to make CQ[*6] calls throughout the following days, and continued to fail. My optimism faded accordingly. In fact, all sensory experience seemed to fade in those early days once routines were established. Very quickly, the whir of whistling wind and the humming throb of diesel engines became the only source of ambient sound – apart from cacophonous engine screeching during the day.

Freezing outdoor temperatures limited body sweat and odour. The only time I recall smelling anything was when there wasn't anything to smell – the smell of being clean after bathing and washing clothes. Throughout the traverse we rinsed socks and jocks routinely. Major ablutions occurred only a few times during our months away.

A monotonously flat horizon filled the prime mover windscreen for most of the journey. Our eyes became finely tuned to the search for indiscernible snow poles located every few kilometres – the only objects higher than one metre along the entire route. Above us, the insipid sun circled above the horizon (mostly). Daylight was exceeded only by the overabundance of ice and snow. Both a necessity and a curse, daylight facilitated overland travel at any hour of the day, but also disrupted sleep patterns.

Friday 23 December 1983:

We arrived at ice movement station and traverse marker GM01 to discover a quaint wooden sign displaying the name of my supervisor, one of the three previous Australian glaciologists to participate in a Dome C traverse. GM01 was my first remeasurement task apart from the pole at Vostok. And, because of that terrible experience, I proceeded at a snail's pace, spending 1.5 hours to meticulously unpack and assemble the JMR.

Throughout the day, our two tractor trains often separated by several kilometres, at times out of sight with each other due to ground drift. The 35-tonne Kharkovchanka towed a fuel sled and stores sled. The

---

6. CQ resembles the first two syllables of the French word 'sécurité' for 'pay attention' and/or 'c'est qui', meaning in French 'who's there?'.

ATT – meaning in English 'heavy artillery tractor' – towed the balok only. The Kharkovchanka was a special Antarctic vehicle built on a modified ATT platform. Kharkovchanka means literally, 'the little lady from Kharkov city'. The first part of the word refers to the city of Karkov (or Kharkiv), the second largest city in Ukraine where the vehicle was constructed. The suffix 'chanka' means 'little lady'.

Five Kharkovchankas constructed between 1974 to 1976 were deployed to Antarctica by the Soviet Antarctic Expedition, four of them to Mirny. Two supported the Dome B traverse, one supported our Dome C traverse. Another supported the Vostok resupply traverse. The fifth was based at another Soviet station – Novolazarevskaya on the South African side of Antarctica. The Kharkovchanka had a rated towing capacity of 60 tonnes and a nominal top speed of 30 km/h. It featured an integrated living van in place of the ATT's cargo tray. The living area contained bunks for three people.

Our balok, designed and built by a commercial aircraft manufacturer, featured compartmentalised rooms for sleeping/dining, food preparation, radio operations and power generation. The sleeping/dining space contained a large central timber table surrounded by sets of double bunks to accommodate six or seven people.

The 20-tonne ATT was a rugged military vehicle based on the design of a Soviet T-54 tank. Within the Soviet Union the ATT towed or carried cannons, guns, ammunition and heavy equipment. For our traverse it towed either the balok or the fuel sled. Our one and only fuel sled supplied both prime movers from a dual compartment bulk tank of 30-tonne capacity. An electric pump system removed the otherwise labour-intensive task of hand pumping fuel from 200-litre drums, as we did on Australian Antarctic traverses. Despite fitting a new engine to the ATT prior to departure, the vehicle was not thoroughly tested and malfunctioned from day two. Horrified by the obvious implications, Serge and Valery immediately contacted the returning Vostok traverse hoping to swap our suspect machine, to no avail.

Saturday 24 December 1983:

By mid-morning we'd caught up to the Dome B team, station-ary at an agreed spot, waiting to rendezvous with the peloton of returning Vostok tractor trains.

Two faster vehicles from the Vostok team had raced ahead and already reached Mirny. Two ATTs were under tow. Despite depleted numbers, the arriving convoy was an awesome spectacle, rumbling in one tractor train at a time in a cloud of fog and swirling drift snow. The katabatic wind* blew loose snow ahead of the vehicles producing the weird appearance of vehicles moving backwards in the subdued light. As the vehicles stopped moving, the men leaped out. They introduced themselves to comrades old and new. Hugs, vig-orous conversation and boisterous toasts followed. Several wrestled playfully in the snow. I was immediately introduced to Mikhail – a Vostok winterer and mechanic, amateur radio enthusiast and reason-ably fluent English speaker. He expressed interest in operating the Astro C, which he already knew about. Unfortunately, my 12-volt batteries were discharged and not capable of powering the radio.

During the afternoon, Vlad drew my attention to an arriving tractor train: 'See those 44-gallon drums over there' he said, 'the ones being towed behind vehicles ... Vodka!' All personnel moved indoors for dinner at 9pm. Rendezvous celebrations escalated, fuelled by litres of vodka. At one stage I counted 29 or 30 men jammed into one balok, a space designed to comfortably accommodate eight around the dinner table. Being crammed in like sardines was perfect for the Russian personal space ethos. It also maintained cosy warmth. Colleagues commonly draped an arm around each other, with faces so close the lips and nose almost touched. I realised this was cus-tomary, but my Anglo-Saxon values felt compromised. The evening raged with raucous singing and solo dancing, both in the aisles and on the spot. We launched into Christmas dinner with an entrée of salmon, sardines, smoked fish, chillies and bread followed by soup, fish and cooked buckwheat. Rather unusually, the conversation and noise intensified upon the arrival of the main course. Throughout the celebrations, but particularly after dinner, a solitary guitar made its way around, available for random strumming by anyone capable, accompanied by the rowdy noise of inebriated choristers.

We sang one favourite repeatedly and loudly, a popular, blokey Russian folk song called 'Father Frost', which began 'Oi moroz moroz ... Nee moroz meenya ... nee moroz meenyah ... moesha kon.' The lyrics (translated in English) went:

> *Oh frost, frost*
> *Don't freeze me*
> *Don't freeze me*
> *And my horse*
>
> *And my horse*
> *My white-maned horse*
> *I have a wife*
> *Oh, she is jealous*
>
> *I have a wife*
> *Oh, she is a beauty*
> *She waits for me at home*
> *She waits, she is grieving for me*
>
> *I am coming to her*
> *At the sunset of the day*
> *I will embrace my wife*
> *And I will groom my horse*

Another aspect of traverse-life that I watched with interest, but stayed well away from, were occasional arm-wrestling contests. Arm wrestling occurred usually, after dinner, but sometimes also literally during dinner. Proponents would often niggle each other at meal-times then, after gulping down the remainder of their food, roll up their shirt sleeves, sweep aside the dirty dishes and lock arms over the table, egged on by others eager to see whether either combatant would yield before breaking an arm.

Sunday 25 December 1983:

I could only think about Kerry. What was she up to?

I couldn't make contact for our first Christmas as a married couple! For me, this was a workday like any other. I knew Kerry felt stressed and abandoned and I hoped family and friends might compensate for my absence. I could do little apart from keep her in my thoughts.

Many of the inbound Vostok tractor trains moved off before we surfaced, keen to access station facilities after months in the field. For those of us heading outbound, intense hangovers provided a convenient excuse to sleep-in. We fired flares to celebrate Christmas and departed in convoy with the Dome B team. We travelled through the afternoon to arrive in the vicinity of GM03 at 9pm, then parted company. The Dome B team continued ahead while we went off to search for the ARMS. Sergey prepared Christmas turkey 'specially for me', he said. Dinner featured delicacies from Mawson – cashews, peanut butter and tomato sauce. I provided the dessert of homemade Christmas cake, made by my mum and devoured ravenously by the team, accompanied by a mug of Earl Grey tea.

Monday 26 December 1983:

The balance of the crew continued a foot search for the ARMS and JMR reference pole (GM03) walking effortlessly across an unusually soft, smooth surface devoid of sastrugi*. Snow conditions at this location were caused by a rare combination of spring snowfalls and gentle breezes. I stayed back to gather a snow sample, and to ensure my scientific equipment was operational by late afternoon.

My first opportunity to contact Earl in Frankston, with whom I'd arranged a 'sked' before leaving Australia, offered the perfect opportunity to contact Kerry. Working chirpily, I set up a V-antenna, fully confident Earl would be listening, but then discovered a broken balun which I could not repair before the scheduled time. I consequently failed to make contact. Another opportunity missed! Dinner consisted of a modest but satisfying meal of pan-fried steak with pasta.

Tuesday 27 December 1983:

I didn't sleep well, kept awake by thunderous snoring. 'Looks like I'll spend the next three months with cotton wool in my ears.'

In Antarctica, snoring is a problem exacerbated by fatigue, cold weather, poor hydration and smoking. Members of Mawson's three-man sledging party on their way to the South Magnetic Pole, for instance, famously recorded frustrations of disrupted sleep from each other's snoring. On this expedition, another equally delicate matter that seemed to affect me more than others was the unbearably hot interior of the Kharkovchanka. Valery (mechanic) explained, 'Heating come from recirculating engine fluid … cannot be adjusted … cannot be disconnected.' Desperate for relief, I examined the interior van fittings carefully and discovered, to my delight, a vent and fan within the dome window of the ceiling, and a power outlet nearby. By opening the vent and operating the fan I could adjust the interior temperature quite accurately! Unfortunately, my discovery was not welcomed by my hosts, who made their preferences clearly known.

We travelled continuously for 24 hours to the next overnight destination at GM04. A brief lunch stop occurred en route, during which we chomped down baked beans and tinned corned beef. It tasted fabulous, mainly because we were very tired, cold and hungry (as usual).

My remarks about cabin temperature triggered a delayed response from my colleagues involving guidance on 'how to dress' and 'how I should arrange my equipment and gear'. I was chastised about 'how to shut doors properly'. Mostly humorous taunts, the comments implied I lacked experience in polar conditions – perhaps forgetting that I had previously spent 12 months in Antarctica. This annoyed me at the time, as did the occasional tendency to speak 'at me' like a caveman if I struggled to follow the verbal discourse. Instead of slowing down, the conversations directed to me sometimes warped into loud, stultifying language, even more difficult to follow. Thankfully, this didn't happen often. Vlad would nearly always jump in and translate. For 99% of the time, interpersonal relations were cordial and respectful. Arguments flared on occasions, mostly when individuals were bored or edgy, or affected by stressful events. I tried to avoid verbalising impolite remarks by scribbling in my notebook. I rationalised, 'I can always tear it up later, but a thoughtless word could be difficult if not impossible to withdraw.'

I wasn't alone or unique in this regard. The crew of Adrien de Gerlache's Belgica expedition of 1898 wrote antagonistic letters to each other from adjacent cabins while stranded during winter in circuitous drift in Graham Land. The major contention was tension between those aiming to perform rigorous science and those partaking in adventure for the sake of adventure. Members of Shackleton's, Scott's and Mawson's expeditions recorded brutal assessments of each other in their personal notebooks, often documented with scathing language. Roald Amundsen's book *My Life as an Explorer* contains withering assessments of almost every person with whom he dealt. After returning to Mirny having spent several months in close proximity, and putting to one side minor irritations caused by personal habits and/or peculiar mannerisms, interpersonal relationships remained cordial and respectful. All team-members remained on good terms with each other, arguably our greatest achievement.

Meanwhile, the local surface conditions had deteriorated. Metre-high, rock-hard sastrugi produced a hellish ride for passengers in the rear of the Kharkovchanka. I changed across to ride in the balok during the day, where it was less noisy, but still rough. Passengers in the balok were thrown around like ragdolls in a washing machine – every moment a surprise. Our drivers did their best but did not suffer like the passengers – being up front with a grab bar available and able to see what was coming, they could brace accordingly.

The large, heavy Soviet vehicles did not have a bulldozer blade like Australian Caterpillar D5 dozers. Soviet vehicles relied on the crushing weight of crawler tracks to flatten sastrugi. Australian dozers, on the other hand, used the blade to knock the tops off sastrugi and smooth a pathway for following sleds – similar to the way grooming machines prepare downhill ski-runs. When travelling through patches of rough sastrugi, the balok would lurch, bump, pitch and twist, then skew to the side every now and then, especially when the prime mover paused to change gears. The tow cable would often snap into tension and jerk the van forward. Occasionally the balok would tip forward as if falling into a huge hole, then jolt out like a surfer paddling through an incoming wave.

Wednesday 28 December 1983:

My 30th birthday at GM04! We arrived at 3:30am for a half hour stopover – barely time for a photograph before continuing on to the last known position of the ARMS station – supposedly 7 km to the east. Our initial search failed to confirm its location. A route-marker revealed itself after a relentless search, but the ARM station remained unidentified. We took a short rest before Vlad and a smaller party set off again.

In the meantime, I collected a snow sample, rearranged equipment and repaired a rope on the flagpole so I might hoist the V-antenna. Before dinner we rummaged through our provisions to select Vegemite and steak sauce as condiments for our meal of chicken and rice. My comrades loved Vegemite! They spread it thickly on everything from ham to cheese. They relished the strong flavour. Similarly, they loved the steak sauce and smothered it over all meals, especially chicken.

I received two gifts for my birthday from traverse colleagues. The first, a handy guidebook to the world-famous art museum, the Hermitage, written in English and personally autographed. I still have it decades later but have not yet visited the Hermitage. The other was more practical: a pair of padded overalls. But the most important gift for which I had hoped was not delivered – an opportunity to talk to Kerry.

Thursday 29 December 1983:

The location of the ARMS remained undiscovered despite an extensive foot search. We widened the search perimeter and engaged the Kharkovchanka to assist. For no particular reason other than convenience, the team voted to adjust watches to Moscow time.

During the morning, while sitting in the balok in silence, an unexpected roar erupted outside. I was shocked. A microsecond of hesitation preceded uproar from my colleagues, who obviously expected something. I wondered whether I'd missed an item of general conversation, because I had no prior expectations. My colleagues jumped to their feet, shouting 'Samalyet!' – airplane! We rushed outside to the sight of an IL14 roaring by on a return flight from Vostok – a perfect day for Antarctic aviation. Our thermometer was almost off the scale, reading between -5°C to -10°C. We waved like maniacs as it made three passes, each pass at ever lower altitudes. The event occurred so quickly I didn't have time to fetch my camera. On the third and final pass a small parcel came tumbling out of the passenger door, about 10 m above the surface. We sprinted over to collect it. A thick blanket bound with string protected the contents from damage. Inside the parcel we found three rubber generator drive belts plus a small note and two other items – a birthday present consisting of a scarf and pair of thick socks addressed to me from Oleg – plus a teapot. *Nice, practical!* I thought. The birthday surprise explained why I was unaware of the IL14's visit beforehand.

Equally welcome, the teapot added immeasurably to our under-whelming range of kitchen utensils and crockery. Until then we had brewed tea in a screw-top glass jar.

Friday 30 December 1983:

My difficulty maintaining charge on the 12V batteries (to operate the JMR and radio) continued, but I had discovered the cause. The Kharkovchanka power generator was delivering a waver-ing voltage output down to 200 volts, instead of maintaining a steady 240-volt output. Instead of charging the batteries, the vehicle was discharging my batteries! Thereafter, I would only use the balok genset, but this meant toting two monstrously heavy marine-grade batteries across several hundred metres of rough sastrugi. We feasted again. Macaroni for breakfast, macaroni for lunch. Macaroni, macaroni, macaroni, macaroni, macaroni! Our staple food!

I also set up the V-antenna for the second time, hoping to contact Earl. Once again, variable output power wreaked havoc with the quality of my radio transmissions. I noticed Vlad also having diffi-culties operating his theodolite, which triggered my suspicions about the cause of the JMR malfunction. I began thinking that these prob-lems may be caused by violent shaking from rough travel across the sastrugi, day after day. At 9pm we set off through the night (figura-tively speaking, since it didn't get dark), travelling until 2am, before halting for New Year's Eve – a major event on our social calendar.

Saturday 31 December 1983:

A rest day of sorts and reasonably warm at -8°C. The wind blew at a stinging 10 to 20 knots.

The team shared housekeeping duties by tidying the balok, sweeping the floor, setting the table and so on, in preparation for the forth-coming revelry. We manufactured banners proclaiming 'S novim godom' – Happy New Year – and strung them round the bunkbeds.

Sergey led meal preparations while the rest of us luxuriated in the warmth of the genset room. One by one we took a proxy banya by melting a pan of snow on the genset motor. Once the water was sufficiently warm, we'd strip off, sponge our body then re-use the tepid leftovers to rinse personal clothing, most importantly socks and jocks. For the first time in the two weeks since departure, each of us looked clean and smelled clean. Unfortunately, the process of taking a banya induced chronic lethargy. All of us reported a strong desire to lie down and sleep. For me, the banya was also an opportunity to assess my injuries. My blackened right eye and the gash on the crown of my head had largely healed. A new red patch had emerged on my forehead. A deep bruise had also emerged on my bum. Fortunately, I wasn't in pain.

We gathered in the balok to prepare dinner ingredients. Slava ground peppercorns on the dining table using the flat side of an axe head. Others, seated on stools in a circle, peeled potatoes into large basins and gossiped. Serge climbed onto the roof of the living van to retrieve frozen meats from storage containers. The meat was thawed in preparation for cooking. We selected, opened and plated a range of tinned accompaniments. Slava strummed the guitar as predinner drinks emerged. The relaxed mood encouraged smoking and the balok filled quickly with choking fumes. I couldn't breathe, but at least we had a fabulous mood.

Smoking continued at epidemic levels throughout the traverse, just like it was at home in the Soviet Union! According to online forums such as the Mayo Clinic, smokers constitute 50% to 60% of the adult male population in today's Russian Federation. Within our team of nine, seven were smokers. The combination of dry air, continuous smoking and runny noses resulted in unconstrained sniffing, and throaty phlegm-busting coughing and spitting. The 'Belomorkanal' brand 'papirosa' was the cigarette of choice. A hollow cardboard tube extended by three to four centimetres with tobacco-filled paper, acted as a disposable cigarette holder and provided constriction to control airflow. The smoker flattened the tube with fingers or teeth while using fingers on the opposite hand to squeeze the tube before lighting up – all part of the theatre of smoking. Papirosa were cheap, strong, unfiltered, quirky and high in tar. Archetypically Russian, papirosa are unlike anything manufactured in the West since World War 2. I am a non-smoker, but nevertheless brought one packet home as a souvenir. It sat in my drawer for several years until eventually I threw it in the bin, where all cigarettes belong.

The New Year celebration commenced officially at 7pm. We hopped into appetisers and toasts, vodka and the occasional nip of double-strength vodka prior to wolfing down a bottle of Johnny Walker Red and one bottle of homebrew whisky made by Valentine G. A drawn-out speech prefaced each toast. Normally the speech explained the detailed context for the toast while listeners waited with arms extended, glass at the ready. Typically, the toast developed to a crescendo followed by the outcry 'Na zdorovye' (Your health)! Sometimes I'd chip in with 'Cheers'. We paid tribute to the New Year at Mirny, to the New Year in Melbourne, to the New Year in Moscow, to the New Year in Australia, to comrades at other Antarctic stations, to our leaders, to ourselves, to people at home, to war heroes, to towns generally, our wives, parents, friends, partners, world peace and so on. Any reason was good reason.

The main course presented by chef Sergey consisted of 'zharennaya kartoshka' (fried potatoes) with chicken, followed by rehydrated ice-cream and the last of my mum's fruitcake. New Year's dinner was tasty, filling and unsophisticated. We drank like fish and ate like Skuas*. We sang like an inebriated Welsh choir and consumed the best of our meagre rations. Drinking vessels varied. The more conventional included a screw-top glass jar and enamel mug. I commandeered an empty Vegemite glass – the kind with a metal lid that you levered off that is no longer produced – before my comrades realised its potential as a robust drinking tumbler. We only started with two jars of Vegemite. Once their value was realised, each jar was opened immediately, the contents devoured, containers washed, and the glasses hidden under a mattress. The alternatives were clear. If I intended to claim one as a matter of cultural appropriation, I'd have to wrestle for it. Needless to say, I never touched either of them again. They probably ended up in Moscow.

The new year's formalities wound up as the clock reached 12 midnight Moscow time. We fired flares to celebrate, then called it a night.

Sunday 1 January 1984:

Back to work. We travelled to a new location 10 km west of GM017, following the tracks of preceding Vostok tractor trains. The pleasant weather, manifested by temperatures between -10°C to -15°C, with visibility to the horizon and light winds of 5 to 10 knots, contrasted starkly with an uneven surface of high sastrugi and a very rough ride. I found it difficult to concentrate or relax but occupied time reading, as best I could, An Indecent Obsession by Colleen McCulloch. The continuous crashing over the rough surface was totally exhausting, evidenced by a sombre mood at dinner.

Monday 2 January 1984:

Today's destination, ARMS station S61, approximately 355 km from Mirny at an elevation of 2,600 m, marked 11 full days since departure. Averaging 30 km/day, with an estimated 1,500 km distance from Mirny to Dome C, we needed to move faster to achieve our target duration of six weeks each way. I established a JMR measurement station at Vlad's request to provide coordinates for the magnetic field station. The position marker was useful for navigation, but since I was likely to be the last person

*with a satellite doppler receiver passing this way for some time,
if ever, it was unlikely to be remeasured for glaciology purposes.*

Moderate weather prevailed, the air temperature a tolerable -19°C, which in the absence of wind and humidity was comfortable without a hat or mitts. I basked in the sun dressed in a shirt, trousers and jumper only, feeling warm if the sun was shining on my back. The sun 'warming factor' was rather like reverse 'windchill'. I did wear gloves at times, mainly to prevent my sweaty hands from sticking to, or being zapped by, the metal door handles.

Limited ingredients and a lack of kitchen utensils encouraged monotonous meals. Our dinner comprised spaghetti with tinned corned beef, black tea, and bread spread thickly with rich, delicious blackcurrant jam.

Onward to Dome C

Tuesday 3 January 1984:

Departure occurred the minute ARMS maintenance finished, at 3:30pm Moscow time. We arrived at our next stop, the unmanned Soviet inland station Pionerskaya, at 8pm Moscow time. Pionerskaya is located one-third of the straight-line distance between Mirny and Vostok. Protruding snow poles and antennas indicated the precise location of the old buildings that lay buried in drift snow. Abandoned vehicles littered the area. The remnants of a large French/Soviet snow surface strain grid also remained visible.

The surface strain grid consisted of timber and metal poles set in a square cross over a distance of kilometres, against which distance was measured over time to assess ice surface deformation rate; that is, the process by which glaciers and ice sheets flow. While travelling during the day, I programmed the JMR with alerts based on satellite arrival times that depended on our exact latitude and longitude. In 1983, only a handful of satellites were accessible for non-military applications. Some did not orbit with an orientation suitable for Antarctic regions. An accurate position fix to within, say, a metre or two, typically required two days' worth of satellite passes.

We had another late night, this time outdoing each other with magic tricks. My trick involved identifying a coin with the head (or tail) side up from beneath the hands of a chosen participant. The process went like this. I would ask a participant to place two coins on the table, one with its head up, the other tail-side up. After covering my eyes with a blindfold or hands (or both) I would turn away then ask the participant to move the coins around. Next, I would request the participant place one hand on their head and the other on their tail and leave them there without changing position while I counted from one to ten. Before removing the blindfold and opening my eyes, I would ask the participant to take the hand on their head and place it on top of the coin with the head side up, and the hand on their tail on top of the coin with the tail-side up.

The magic occurred during the next stage. After removing my blindfold to face the participant with my eyes open, I would raise fingers to my brow, look down, close my eyes, concentrate and squint to ingest cosmic energy. I usually needed several seconds, but not too long, to synchronise with the brainwaves of my volunteer. Well, that's what I told them. I could only announce a decision when sure (usually by asking the others) if the participant had followed the instructions. If they had, I always correctly identified the nominated coin (head or tail). By doing this correctly time after time (say 10 times in a row) my audience was impressed and graciously agreed to abide by the magician's creed to not pressure me into divulging details. I doubt I would have fooled a real magician.[7]

---

7. Raise one arm above your head and simultaneously lower the other arm to your side. Hold the position for ten seconds then place both hands next to each other on a table under good light. Look carefully at your hand colour. Can you notice a difference? Magic! All the rest is nonsense.

Clearly my magic had evaporated when I next attempted transmissions with the amateur radio. I spent ages setting up the V-antenna, only to find I had insufficient power from either the Kharkovchanka or my 12-volt batteries. 'The Astro C is a white elephant,' I diarised. But the magic returned when we commenced moving. The 28-volt vehicle supply stabilised, and although the incoming signal was weak, I could nevertheless hear transmissions over the top of incessant engine noise.

Initially, the incoming broadcasts were incoherent. I persevered until conditions improved, eventually contacting amateurs in Japan and several parts of Africa. Contact with Mawson, Casey and Australia remained impossible. I put out CQ calls inviting Earl to respond, but the minute I uttered, 'This is VK0AG,' the zero revealed my location as Antarctica and amateur radio enthusiasts went nuts, flooding me with requests to exchange QSL cards.*[8]

After this breakthrough, I attempted on numerous occasions and finally succeeded at operating while mobile. Some operators seemed to be scanning and trolling for my CQ calls because they made repeated contact. Each time I explained that I couldn't respond because I wouldn't be back in Australia for months. However, by the time I returned home I had 50 QSL cards waiting from operators all over the world. Many originated from Japan where the skip distance* and time zone for my location in Antarctica was ideal. Others contacted me from bizarre locations, including Chicago, Moscow, Hong Kong, Berlin, Monaco, Bulgaria, Sweden, New Zealand, Knoxville Tennessee, the Netherlands and Czechoslovakia. Two QSL cards came from Australia, including one from Tasmania. This occurred more than a decade before the availability of email or text messages. During my time in the field Kerry may not have been able to speak to me often, but at least she knew I was alive from the incoming stream of QSL cards mailed to my registered call sign address.

---

8. Today's equivalent of a QSL card is a Facebook friend.

Engine noise reverberating inside the Kharkovchanka caused difficulties hearing incoming radio transmissions while mobile, and even more difficulties for my outgoing transmissions. I hoped one of the Valentines may have a headset squirrelled away, or an innovative solution for dampening the ambient noise. Unfortunately, they did not. Both were electronics specialists; both were eager to pull the Astro C apart to investigate the American technology. They frequently heckled me about the 'dainty and fragile' Astro C, which of course it wasn't. It was incredibly heavy and robust, but maybe too high-tech for polar conditions.

Wednesday 4 January 1984:

A rest day. Most of the team, except me, slept till mid-afternoon. I couldn't due to the snoring, occasional whinnies, 'ooohs' and 'aaahs' and sniffing. The snoring drove me crazy. I tried everything to block it out: pillows over my head, cotton wool in my ears, anything I could think of, mostly to no avail. If only before leaving Australia someone had suggested I take earmuffs and a bag full of ear plugs!

During the afternoon we formed a ravioli production line, chatting while we produced the little meat parcels wrapped in pasta. That meal was better than anything I'd tasted from the kitchen at Mirny. Somehow the discussion turned to Antarctic remuneration. Vlad mentioned how Soviet 'field personnel' received a 25% loading while away from the station. Mental note: Australians did not receive this allowance! Daytime temperatures hovered around -20°C to -21.5°C.

Thursday 5 January 1984:

JMR-1 ran smoothly at GM05. I gathered 60 satellite passes, more than enough for an accurate position measurement.

Local sastrugi were not as high or rough compared with other parts through which we'd travelled. This assisted our ride in a manner comparable to sailing in following seas. Sastrugi are like crescent-shaped sand dunes on a small scale. They self-generate under the action of prevailing winds and blowing snow. Although sastrugi were a powerful menace, their orientations were useful as a navigation aid. We followed an existing pole line, but between poles (which at best were kilometres apart and difficult to spot in heavy drift) sastrugi provided a steering reference similar to the way in which swell direction or coastal features provide a point of reference for ocean sailors steering yachts.

Another interesting surface feature, albeit less obvious most of the time, was the visible surface hills and valleys generated by the ice as it flowed coastward in a dampened and displaced harmonic of crustal features far below. On average, the icesheet is kilometres thick and mostly overlies mountainous bedrock. While it is tempting to think of the icesheet as static and immovable, nothing could be further from the truth. The wavelength of surface undulations across Antarctica varies but is typically between 5 km to 15 km, an effect similar to a standing wave (or stationary wave) in a river rapid.

To date I had travelled mostly in the rear of the Kharkovchanka, or the balok, without disembarking until the end of a day's travel. Now, I needed to take snow accumulation readings at snow poles every two kilometres for the remainder of the trip, through to Dome C. This meant hopping off and back onto the vehicles at 10-minute intervals. After a small discussion, we agreed I should ride up front in the cabin of the ATT to help spot upcoming poles and minimise lost time at stoppages. The ATT towed a lighter load and could handle frequent stops, whereas the Kharkovchanka could not.

Refuelling plus the need to replace broken track pins for both prime movers delayed our departure from GM05 until 4:30pm, pushing out our arrival time at ice movement station GM06 to 10:30pm 'Moscow time'.

Friday 6 January 1984:

From GM06 we travelled 80 km to reach ice movement station GM07, placing us 120 km from Pionerskaya. The continuing fine weather and snow conditions (for most of the journey thus far) had allowed the ATT to maintain an average speed of 10 km/hr. In contrast, the heavier Kharkovchanka with heavier tow loads, could only achieve 7 km/hr at best.

Saturday 7 January 1984:

I collected a large set of satellite passes at GM07 despite it being a low priority remeasurement station. The JMR cranked steadily while Slava and I tramped 4 km around the accumulation grid to remeasure stake heights. I collected a snow sample then lay down utterly exhausted.

Over dinner, two colleagues expressed interest in receiving some of my possessions – should I be looking to give them away. Some were personal items, others were pieces owned by the Antarctic Division. During the coming weeks, I received further light-hearted teasing about the 'poor quality' of my clothing, my gloves, batteries, multimeter, tools, CD player: pretty much all of my chattels – a tactic intended to cajole me into giving things away. I wondered whether they really wanted this stuff, or whether it was simply a game.

Sunday 8 January 1984:

The science measurements continued for a second day. We stayed put as the weather deteriorated. Temperatures sank to around -22°C to -28°C. The wind started to bite, blowing steadily at 15 to 20 knots, driving larger volumes of snowdrift.

I successfully activated the Astro C after discovering an electronic short between the tuner lead and the mount for the whip antenna. Although failing to contact Earl and hoping to talk to Kerry, I did make contact with an Australian called John in Mt Waverley. Due to a combination of static and fading signal I struggled to communicate effectively but managed to ask John to ring Kerry, and to also let Earl know I was on the air and okay. I requested John advise Earl of my hope to make contact the following day. I marvelled at contact with someone so close to home and was delighted by further news that during my time on air, vehicle generator repairs were completed successfully and now I could be confident of reliable power going forward.

I continued to experiment with amateur radio for much of the afternoon but couldn't break through with a transmission. One conversation I overheard involved an operator in the US and another in Australia discussing employment opportunities with NASA and the Space Shuttle project. At least this confirmed the whip antenna worked and the possibility of being able to chat to Australia while mobile. Plus, I diagnosed the fault with the V-antenna and made repairs by soldering a loop to the end of each antenna wire.

Monday 9 January 1984:

I contacted Earl for a second consecutive day. John had obviously relayed my message as requested. My parents drove across town to join Earl after they too received notice I would be on air.

However, Kerry was the person I most wanted to contact. She was at Queenscliff for several days with work colleagues, and not due home till Friday. Bugger! In those days the absence of mobile phones prevented spontaneous arrangements. It seemed unlikely Kerry and I would catch up for our wedding anniversary, now just days away on 14 January. I missed talking to her at Christmas. I missed her again on my birthday. A conversation over amateur radio, although terribly public, was the best way (the only way) I could hope to celebrate.

We travelled all day in whiteout to reach 'pole 95', approximately 190 km from Pionerskaya. During lunch (at 9pm summertime in Australia), I called in for a scheduled contact with Earl. Initial conditions were scratchy but improved towards the middle of our conversation. Earl switched antennas. He fired up a linear amplifier to improve reception. 'Kerry is still away,' he said. I remained optimistic, still hoping to connect at the weekend.

For Kerry, the Christmas/New Year period was dismal. Her parents and sister visited from Sydney and stayed at our home in Mt Eliza. Kerry fought to hold back tears much of the time. Our friends Rod and Bonnie dropped in unannounced on Christmas morning on their way to Phillip Island. Rod sat down, ate six mince pies, then they both left. It's funny what you remember, which in Kerry's case was, and still is, everything! Earl and I chatted for an hour despite poor propagation conditions. Our conversation repeated a familiar theme: 'say again, over ... sorry, say again.' The repetition affected the quality but not the excitement of the banter, it added excitement. Amateur radio was great if things worked out. After Earl, I tried unsuccessfully to contact Ron at Casey. Vlad was also a licensed amateur radio operator and had spoken to Ron earlier. I suspect he had responded to an incoming CQ call possibly intended for me.

We ceased travelling at 9pm. Vlad updated me about an incident in the Kharkovchanka earlier in the day, involving the JMR. One of the battery power cables had overheated and melted the vinyl benchtop. Fortunately, Vlad spotted the problem and acted quickly to disconnect the cables before serious damage occurred. Meanwhile, exposure to noise while travelling in the cabin of the ATT was causing me significant tinnitus at the end of each day. When we ceased driving, I would climb down from the cabin and immediately notice my ears were ringing and humming, typically for half an hour. The cabin noise was so loud we had to shout to be heard. None of us had hearing protection. I did try stuffing my ears with cotton wool. It made no difference. The racket was unbelievable.

My companions reported feeling drained and exhausted every day. Altitude was partly to blame. Simply moving was tiring, exacerbated by the long work hours and decreasing temperatures as we climbed to higher altitudes. Hammering track pins caused the quickest onset of fatigue. It was hard physical work, like chopping wood. It exercised muscles in the back, shoulders and arms 'you didn't know you had'. Wherever possible, we 'hammered' standing upright, working the arms like a pendulum. The method of removing broken pins and inserting new pins depended on the location of the pin. Sometimes you needed to wield the hammer, lying on your back or side directly on the snow surface, using arm action only.

We had previously requested and hoped for an airdrop of new cable for the winch at the front of the ATT. The drivers had radioed through their request days earlier, with the aircraft scheduled to arrive tomorrow between 6am and 8am. Soviet Antarctic stations enjoyed an enviable range of mobile plant and machinery, including gigantic prime movers and robust ski-equipped airplanes, but they had limited tools and almost no spare parts. This wasn't new or different for my year. I knew I could expect this before leaving Australia. Accordingly, prior to departure I had assembled a range of small tools and consumables that I considered necessary to be self-sufficient in my own role. My collection of small tools included a soldering iron, multigrips, screwdrivers, jeweller screwdrivers, pliers, logbooks, batteries, cable connectors, a selection of nuts and bolts, insulated copper wire, fuses, alligator clips, coaxial cable leads, packaging tape, a set of Allen keys, a Stanley knife, scissors, adjustable spanners, side-cutters, a battery charger and charging leads, a 240-volt extension lead, a distribution board, octopus straps, several tape measures, one file, a multimeter and a long wire radio antenna wrapped on a fishing reel. A number of additional items I overlooked would have made a huge difference, a hygrometer, for example, and battery load test meter to monitor charge. Other regrettable omissions included a hand drill and drill set, metric open-ended ring spanners and a pair of longneck pincers to help diagnose and repair problems with the JMR. But who would have thought I'd be doing that?

Tuesday 10 January 1984:

We travelled on. Another 70 km gained to GM16, approximately 260 km east of Pionerskaya. Course direction into the prevailing wind meant fewer bumps from the wedge-shape sastrugi, although the surface texture remained pretty rough. We continually monitored distance travelled, mindful of the requirement to return to base by mid-March. With significantly less fuel to haul on the return trip and fewer stops for the science program, we estimated a 30% improvement in average daily distance (to around 90 to 100 km per day) could be achieved.

Familiar, although tedious, daily routines ensured we never went hungry. Regularly spaced meals and rest stops combined with a high carb diet protected our health and assisted us to tolerate the cold. Serge (cook) served up macaroni for breakfast, lunch and dinner, alternating with 'kasha' or porridge in several guises as either oatmeal, wheat or rice.

For various reasons I was enjoying this expedition more than my traverse year at Casey. Camaraderie was the main factor, but the inclusion of a dedicated cook and doctor in our team removed significant workload and risk for all team members. Marker poles along most of the route significantly reduced stopping and starting, and thus, the risk of equipment breakage. As well, less physical work was required to install or replace missing poles. We didn't even take snow poles with us.

Similarly, the presence and availability of an electric fuel pump removed the laborious hand pumping I had experienced at Casey where prime movers were refuelled by manual pumping from drums. Here, I could concentrate on science activities with minimal additional duties, apart from hammering track pins, a thankless task, but shared by all. During my year at Casey, our diesel mechanics spent a similar amount of time rewelding broken sled 'kingpins', but with little assistance from others.

Regrettably, heavy ground drift prevented the requested airdrop. I wasn't aware of the reasons why it was necessary to deliver the replacement drum cable, and as events transpired, we carried on successfully without it. The IL14 sat idle on the ground at Komsomolskaya waiting for conditions to improve. After several hours and a deteriorating weather forecast, the aircraft returned to Mirny. To date, issues with broken track pins had slowed progress but we hadn't suffered serious mechanical breakdown – an achievement soon about to change!

Wednesday 11 January 1984:

Valery's discovery of a frozen air filter in the Kharkovchanka caused a delayed start.

I tried to call the AAD Glaciology Section in Melbourne to discuss ongoing problems with the JMR-4, but radio conditions were poor. Then a fuse blew on the power board. I sent an official telegram through Sergey (radio operator), requesting a second sked' for the same time next week, then went back to help hammer track pins. We departed very late at 4pm, causing an even later arrival at an abandoned Soviet drilling site 10 km from GM10. We camped overnight, utterly exhausted. I was so glad this was not an ice movement station and therefore I didn't have to set up that damn JMR.

We also noticed the ATT malfunctioning regularly, mainly due to overheating – not an issue you'd expect in the Antarctic. Then, as if in solidarity, the Kharkovchanka became unserviceable with faulty electrical systems and constant breakages to track pins. Alarm bells were not sounding just yet … not … just … yet!

Thursday 12 January 1984:

The Kharkovchanka got away at 8:30am. Serge (mechanic) and I waited in the ATT for half an hour longer, before commencing travel. A staggered start became the established norm. The ATT travelled faster and would usually overtake the Kharkovchanka

during the day, even with the ATT stopping every two kilome-
tres and a half-hour siesta for us during the middle of the day.

We stopped at GM10 to undertake routine maintenance on the
ARMS. For some reason this took longer than the one to two
hours expected. I used the opportunity to call random colleagues at
Australian Antarctic stations, commencing with Vince at Mawson.
Unfortunately, Vince was not able to chat, preoccupied with packing
personal effects for his demobilisation on 21 January. Next, I contacted Ron at Casey after switching frequencies to 7 MHz. We were
barely able to hear each other. I discontinued the conversation and
then tuned in to overhear Davis personnel talking to an ANARE
stalwart onboard the Australian resupply ship *Nanok S*. Propagation
conditions varied as I jumped around the frequency band. I dropped
into another conversation with Terry at Casey and requested he ask
Ron to come back to me on 14 MHz, not 7 MHz. I was keen to
share my experience and pick up ideas about correcting my problems
with the JMRs, particularly the failure at Vostok. Just as I attempted
to contact Earl, the batteries gave out, but I had at least experienced
an enjoyable hour of conversation and reversed my opinion about the
value of the Astro C.

After completing maintenance at GM10 we bustled into action
again, travelling until 9pm then stopping at a point 40 km from
GM15. One benefit of riding in the ATT cabin was discovering my
companion and driver, Serge (mechanic), to be chatty and sociable,
far more than he appeared within the larger team. Within the larger
group he seemed introverted, perhaps because of his younger age.
He surprised me with a suggestion to help improve my vocabulary.
Each day I 'should choose two new words and practice them in
short conversation', which we did during stops for snow accumulation readings. Serge was patient and set a new trend in the team by
speaking to me slowly in Russian, using simple words, rather than
increasing the volume or turning to Vlad for translation. His attitude

rubbed off on the others, who became gradually more considerate as the traverse progressed.

Serge (mechanic) and I chatted about family, life and military service. In the Soviet Union, for instance, every adult male entered the army at 18 years of age for two years of compulsory military service. I explained that nowadays the Australian Army consisted of volunteers only, but that it hadn't always been so. I explained how the Whitlam Labor government abolished national service (established by the Menzies coalition government in 1964 to boost numbers for the Vietnam War) in December 1972, three weeks before my 19th birthday. Had I been 'called up', I could have and would have deferred due to my university studies. But otherwise, I would have been bound by law to register and thereby find myself at risk of random selection by 'birthday ballot'. At the time Australian young men (men only) selected, or conscripted, served two years full time in the regular army, or three years part time in the reserves.

Another point that Sergey found hard to believe, albeit amusing, was the existence – as I explained it, of fortifications constructed in the 1850s at the entrance to Australian capital cities to protect our country from the perceived threat of Russian invasion. I also described my father's 'war story' of signing up for World War 2, underage at 17, then spending three years as a prisoner of war with the Japanese on the Thai–Burma Railway. On one occasion I tried to converse about politics, but Serge did not show interest. 'What do you think about x, y, z …?' I said. Before uttering a word, he turned towards me, then with an emerging smile held up his greasy blackened hands (including stumpy scarred fingers and chewed nails) and said, 'This is how I think, I do my thinking with these!'

Friday 13 January 1984:

We arrived at GM15 where I set up the JMR and programmed satellite arrival times to automatically power-up the JMR. The JMR would then record doppler data on cassette tapes for

*computer processing on return to Australia. Achieving data for
an accurate position fix was quick on this occasion. I had access
to an unusually high number (five) of tracked US Navy satellites. The temperature outside hovered around -20°C, with light
wind, soft snow conditions and 60 cm high sastrugi.*

Old New Year

At the end of the day's travel, we commenced preparations for a
second New Year's party, an unofficial Soviet celebration of 'Old
New Year' dating back to 1918. After the October Revolution,
Lenin issued a decree: 'Wednesday 31 January 1918 will be followed
by Thursday 14 February 1918.' Lenin's decree brought Russia in line
with the Gregorian calendar and the rest of Europe by eliminating
13 days from the old calendar. Luckily we also needed to stop for
science, so we had free time to toast the revolution!

Our festivities were energetic as usual: abundant singing and
dancing with a measure of alcohol. One of our normally mild-man-
nered team members became unusually animated on this occasion,
unleashing his sizeable frame in a dance frenzy. Leaping in all directions with and without musical accompaniment, he started throwing
his weight around, kicking like a mule at random objects while slapping his thighs, chest and head in Austrian slap dance style, but out
of control. At one point during a rousing chorus, he grabbed my
hand and crushed it. Minutes later he held out his hand asking in
Russian, 'How do you say in English?' Sucked in by what I thought
was contrition, I reached out expecting a handshake and apology,
but instead he wrenched my arm behind my back. Things could have
gone haywire. It was a bit crazy.

As the party warmed up, so did the conversation. Fuelled by
alcohol, another team member who was slurring his words and
slightly off balance, sought my opinion on cultural differences
between Russians and Americans. Sensing the possibility of a verbal

brawl, others intervened 'Uh oh! Whoa … This is too serious,' they said in Russian. Our small group included two card-carrying party members, on par with the national average. Typically, 5% to 10% of the Soviet population belonged to the Communist Party. Some took their affiliations seriously, others did not. One of our card-carrying members was also a Russian's Russian. He didn't like American cigarettes. He wouldn't drink English tea. And, while beating his chest, he would often exclaim, 'Vodka is the only drink for a real man.'

After dodging an awkward discussion about American culture, our conversation moved on to the elections of the Supreme Soviet – a process underway in Russia at the time. A suggestion emerged light-heartedly, 'Perhaps Treeva could vote as well!' After all, I was part of the collective. But the idea didn't progress when our Party Member took umbrage. In Australia we might call it 'branch stacking'; the subject was not mentioned again. We drank vodka and proposed toasts, mostly to ourselves, but not before a quick update on the technique to consume double-strength vodka. The method, we were informed, commenced by expressing a guttural 'arghhhhh' with your eyes screwed up, followed by pursed lips, then … after gulping a shot, chomping down bread with fried salmon (almost straight oil) to soak up the alcohol. The bread and salmon also mitigated against vomiting.

Throughout our celebration, Sergey (cook/magnetologist) performed a self-appointed role as choir master by positioning himself alongside Slava, who was on guitar. Sergey had a powerful voice and tremendous memory for lyrics. At any hint of weakness from the chorus such as fading melody or forgotten words, Serge would chime in with prompts and stage whispers. Every now and then he would leap up and stand Cossack-like with arms akimbo, feet slightly apart, and his head over his left or right shoulder. He would sing at the top of his voice. Sometimes, in theatrical parody, he would raise his chin, throw back his head, then roll-up each shirt sleeve, slowly and dramatically, rocking from one foot to the other as he primed himself to boom over the top of the group singers.

Dog-tired at 11pm, I retired to the Kharkovchanka thinking (incorrectly) that the 'Old New Year' festivities were complete. I dropped off to sleep immediately in the dark and quiet cabin. Suddenly Vlad, Valery and I – all of us – were woken. In the darkness and still semi-comatose, I sensed I was being pelted with something. Vlad later described it as confetti: lollies, sweets and handfuls of muesli. Squinting in the darkness I could barely distinguish the blackened faces gawking at me from within hooded parkas, inches from my face. Several sets of hands appeared, all black, accompanied by a gaudy commotion as the filthy hands wiped grease and charcoal, or whatever it was, all over my face. Valery and Vlad suffered likewise, leaving a huge mess on the floor overnight. I fell asleep again when the ruckus subsided, and we cleaned up next morning. Vlad informed me, 'this is traditional "Old New Year" Russian custom'.

Saturday 14 January 1984:

Valery and Vlad didn't stir 'til midday, by which time I had checked the JMR and gathered snow samples.

I set about cleaning up the mess in the Kharkovchanka. No-one had emerged from the balok. Strange, I thought. I waited for the generator to start, hoping to recharge my Dynapack batteries, but the balok remained eerily quiet. I received news from Valery that apparently the generator had broken down during the night and was unserviceable. Muttering under his breath, Valery ranted and raved about possibly backtracking 40 km to the old drill site to recover an existing serviceable unit and swap it over with our unserviceable generator.

Realising we might be stationery for an extended period, I stirred the Astro C into immediate action, desperate to contact Kerry for our first wedding anniversary (today)! I relied on the whip antenna mounted on the edge of the roof and didn't expect to break through. Amazingly, Earl responded, reporting a strong incoming signal to

Australia. I was thrilled. Earl too was electrified by the connection but only wanted to talk about the 'ground plane arrangements' for the whip antenna. That's all he cared about. 'I dunno …' I said, 'the antenna is mounted on the roof. It's my first wedding anniversary, what can I say!' I wasn't the least bit interested in the technicalities of Antarctic radio propagation at that moment. I wanted to hear from Kerry. But guess what? Kerry wasn't home. Kerry was visiting friends! Commonly, expeditioners can expect events like this to precede a 'Dear John' letter from a wife or girlfriend left behind in Australia, informing the recipient that he is, at his choice, not only thousands of kilometres and months away from home, but also surplus to emotional requirements. Thankfully, I never received such a letter.

The temperature hovered around -22°C all day. In Melbourne, the temperature was 32°C. Kerry wasn't home … I celebrated my first wedding anniversary eating leftover ravioli for dinner. Earl and I arranged a tentative radio sked' for the following day at 10pm AEST.

Sunday 15 January 1984:

The previous night was my worst case ever of 'Big Eye'*(insomnia). Unable to sleep, I sat up till midnight watching voltage gauges for the main battery bank in the Kharkovchanka, paranoid about maintaining power to operate the JMR. As a reward, I became the unwilling audience for a discordant symphony of sniffing, snorting and performance inhalation caused by blocked sinuses, interspersed with thunderous sighs, burps and farts. Was I going crazy? I could not sleep and couldn't say anything without causing offence. The bunks in the Kharkovchanka were small. My colleague's feet encroached into my bunk.

After hours of watching power supply gauges, I switched the JMR power back to parallel 12-volt Dynapack batteries. The Kharkovchanka power output had dropped from 28 volts to 17 volts.

During a satellite pass, the operating JMR pulled down the supply voltage to 11.7. Something wasn't right.

In addition I felt especially cold inside my sleeping bag. Overnight temperatures were slumping to -30°C, then rising to a top of -12°C in the morning sun. The overnight effects of Big Eye triggered another Antarctic side effect known in Australian Antarctic slang as the 'Long Eye'*, which I suffered the entire day.

When the time came to get up and commence work, one of my roommates started reading in a strange and out-of-character event. He lay in his bunk for hours without explanation, while I worked away. I attempted to remain quiet and felt distinctly uncomfortable. Something was wrong and my language wasn't polished enough to enquire without (I thought) inflaming the situation. Was an interpersonal problem playing out? Did we have a major mechanical breakdown? Was some other catastrophe to blame? I couldn't tell, although the reason became clear the following day – something to do with broken valve springs.

Monday 16 January 1984:

We remained stationery while repairs continued on the genset motor. A valve spring had indeed broken. It looked like we might be stationary for one full day at least, so I decided to open JMR04 to investigate the performance issues, hoping to find an obvious fault.

My alternative GPS unit, JMR-1, was also malfunctioning and untrustworthy. Without a serviceable JMR, my science program was kaput, yet we'd barely commenced. With no spare parts, no technical training, no diagnostic tools and no idea how to diagnose electrical circuitry, I approached the two Valentines for help, 'Could either of you assist me?' I realised they could do little more than I could without parts or diagnostic tools, but perhaps they could confirm whether or not my machine was beyond repair. I figured that further damage might be caused if I tried to investigate. On the other hand,

I reasoned, 'these instruments cannot repair themselves. The situation is as desperate as can be. I must do something!'

Given the increasing likelihood of an extended delay to the genset repairs, I opened the lid of the JMR and was shocked by the sight of loose bolts, bare wires and shorting visible as blackened wires. One bolt floated completely loose. I could see numerous cracked and 'dry' soldered joints, which while alarming, were at the same time consoling. Since visiting Vostok I had blamed myself and worried whether I had caused the JMR failure. Now, by simply removing the lid and looking inside, I could understand why the instrument wasn't performing. The broken soldering was most likely caused by vibration and, potentially, rough handling during transport to Antarctica, exacerbated no doubt by the violent shaking throughout the traverse. I thought about the JMR situation over and over. I frequently replayed events in my head while I lay in my bunk at night. I brooded over voyage events and airflights, trying to remember episodes of rough handling, not that I could do anything. After considerable reflection, I decided (in my own mind) that the treatment these instruments received was no worse than the treatment similar machines received during my year at Casey.

To try and salvage the situation I resoldered breaks then tugged gently on accessible connections to identify and resolder less obvious cracks. At completion I tested voltages. They seemed correct but I could not successfully restore normal operations. The exercise did, however, leave me brimming with confidence to be not afraid to strive for positive outcomes, no matter how unlikely. I immediately decided to 'operate' on my 35mm Nikkormat SLR camera. Ever since my crash on the sea ice at Mawson, I'd been troubled by a worsening problem with the camera's film winding mechanism. The camera worked okay immediately after the accident but as we encountered lower temperatures, the winder began sticking and playing up. Now it was totally jammed. I wasn't confident of rectifying the problem, but once again figured that 'this camera cannot repair itself. Unless I investigate, it will be useless to me for the rest of the trip.'

Having removed the film canister, I used jeweller screwdrivers to disconnect and carefully remove the top casing. I spent ages staring at the winding mechanism, advancing the winder and studying the movement and pinch points. Finally, I identified an issue. The winder shaft seemed ever so slightly bent. Aided by a clumsy pair of electrician's pliers – instead of needle nose pliers that would have been far more appropriate, I applied pressure gently to the shaft, then tested the mechanism. I repeated the process over and over by applying gentle pressure to the shaft, then advancing the winder a few times while feeling and looking for the sticking, or pinch point. Eventually I achieved what I had considered impossible. I successfully removed the pinch point. The film winder worked perfectly for the remainder of the expedition. I was so satisfied that I didn't bother sending my camera to Nikon for repair after returning to Australia.

'Victor Kilo Three Lima Gulf, this is Victor Kilo Zero Tango Hotel, how do you read? VK0TH this is VK3LG, I read you 3 by 1. VK3LG this is Victor Kilo Zero Tango Hotel reading you 5 x 5.' At 10:00 GMT* (midday in Australia) Earl contacted me to suggest rescheduling to 11:00 GMT due to interference at his end.

Our second attempt was no different from the previous day. Propagation conditions had not improved. Earl had, however, in the meantime phoned Kerry on the landline – we didn't have mobile phones. Kerry drove to Earl's place hoping for our first proper conversation since the traverse commenced. It was an exciting moment, at least it was for me. As usual, the conversation commenced with spluttering back and forth to determine who could hear whom, similar to a modern day Zoom call without video: 'Can you hear me yet? I can't hear you very well', 'What did you say over? Can you hear me now?' etcetera. We were struggling to connect when a ham operator named Alan chipped in from Sydney. I could hear both of them

5 x 5 (radio lingo for 'loud and clear'). Earl was having difficulty with both of us. Alan could transmit and receive well (5 x 5) with both Earl and me. I would never have thought amateur radio could be so frustrating but at the same time so entertaining! The conditions were patchy at best. Alan offered to relay the conversation between Kerry (via Earl) and me. 'I can hear you and I can hear Trevor,' he said, 'it seems you can't hear each other ... Kerry, is there anything you'd like to say to Trevor?' to which Kerry replied 'Oh ... just say ... I'm missing him, I hope he's safe ... and ... I'm looking forward to him coming home ...'. It wasn't the most intimate conversation, but it was our only available option, so we persisted. I responded by blurting 'Kerry and I have just had our first wedding anniversary shkreeshhh ... sccccratcccccc ... ccccccsssshheeesshhh,' to which Alan improvised as smoothly as silk, 'Kerry ... Trevor sends his undying love,' a statement followed by a drawn-out pause, then a delayed response, followed by another relayed message 'Oh? ... you've obviously got the wrong guy then ...'

Kerry had a tsunami of news. One hour rocketed by as we relayed information to each other. The conversation moved quickly between Christmas celebrations, family movements, swimming achievements, the state of our house, the garden, the vegie patch, our friends. Behind the brave face, Kerry felt lonely and said she was not always feeling the support and encouragement expected from friends and relatives. Earl was accommodating, but Kerry also felt uncomfortable visiting his home in the late evening to talk on the radio. On two later occasions Kerry brought along our next-door neighbour's 14-year-old son, who thought the situation and circumstances were pretty cool – talking on amateur radio to 'the man next door', who was in the Antarctic on a Russian expedition. I thought it was pretty cool too, just quietly! And I was 30 years old!

Tuesday 17 January 1984:

Three weeks have passed since departure. We prepared to camp at GM15 for several days. Excellent weather, clear blue skies, no wind, outside temperature of -25°C. In full sunshine and crispy dry stillness, the temperature didn't feel cold.

A major argument erupted at lunchtime and tempers flared. The context and content of the exchange wasn't clear to me, but it was loud, fierce and emotional. Amazingly, the tension subsided as quickly as it erupted. We continued with lunch (macaroni again and kompot) as if nothing had happened. For dinner we feasted on boiled potatoes accompanied by morsels of fried steak, bread and butter, and a cup of tea. Our location was 20 km past GM15, aiming to reach GM14 tomorrow.

This particular evening, feeling fried by the temperature inside the Kharkovchanka and obviously out-of-kilter with my companions, the stuffiness became overwhelming. I crept out to the vestibule and opened the door for relief. I sat on the entry doorstep with the door ajar for 10 to 15 minutes to escape the sniffing and smoke haze, until inevitably someone yelled out, 'Shut the f...ing door' (in Russian of course).

Wednesday 18 January 1984:

During our lunch stop I made first contact with my supervisor in Australia. Quickly but accidentally, this turned into a five-way conversation between participants at Melbourne Uni, Sydney (Alan, who just happened to be listening), Ron, who at the time was in the field at Lanyon Junction near Casey, and another glaciology colleague operating from Carlton on VK3DH. What an amazing work meeting!

Propagation conditions were excellent. I could hear all of them 5 x 5 as I verbalised my report about the science program, including problems with the JMRs. The conversation morphed into social chit-chat when Alan, a 747–flight engineer in Australia, and Ron, located at Lanyon Junction (at the time installing radar gear for the Casey runway), realised they shared common career interests. Vlad borrowed the microphone for a few minutes to introduce himself. He inquired whether anyone in Australia could shed light on plans by the Americans to fly to Dome C during summer. Someone suggested the US science programs were concentrated at the South Pole and West Antarctica, suggesting further that the Americans were most likely not attending Dome C. Vlad seemed adamant to the contrary but didn't offer context.

Vlad subsequently sent a message to colleagues in Mirny requesting they listen out on 14 MHz for information about US flying activity in Antarctica. He was pressing for details of an opportunity to rendezvous, especially if we could reach the Dome C camp before 1 February. I didn't understand the relevance at the time. Social chit-chat continued for 15 minutes after my supervisor signed off. Vlad seemed impatient to get moving, so we wrapped up, made tracks and travelled through to GM14 for the next overnight stop. I noticed my hands felt cold for the first time since leaving Mirny. The thermometer indicated -37°C, quite a bit colder than previous days, the direct result of our elevation having climbed continuously since leaving the coast.

Thursday 19 January 1984:

I had another conversation with Andrew in Sydney, VK3ATV, who was mobile in a car at Grays Point south of Sydney near the Royal National Park. Unfortunately, Earl didn't respond to my CQ call even though I persisted for 10 minutes, which is when Alan jumped in. I finished my conversation with Alan, expecting the usual flood of incoming CQ calls, but the radio remained unusually quiet.

My bruised ego sought comfort eating familiar foods. On this occasion I was daydreaming about a cup of Earl Grey tea. I trotted over to the balok for a teabag to find (sadly) our stocks had vanished. Plus, the same thing had occurred with the ice-cream, fruitcake and almost all the deli items and groceries from Mawson. Hurrumph! Must be a mice plague!

Woken during the night by an unfamiliar hum that waxed and waned, I lay in my bunk listening and wondering whether I should investigate or simply ignore it. Eventually, I climbed out of my bunk and sleeping bag then dressed while the others remained fast asleep. Outside, I found the cause to be antenna wires vibrating in light breeze, but the noise was hardly audible. Inside the van, harmonic resonance had obviously transmitted through the walls to generate a phenomenal racket, yet it didn't rouse or bother the others. I assumed they had already realised it was nothing serious.

Friday 20 January 1984:

I made strong contact with Earl today and received my first and only telegram from Kerry to advise she was in Sydney! Our lunch stop lasted two hours while waiting for Valery (mechanic) and Sergey (mechanic) to resolve an issue with a frozen oil filter. Calm weather and air temperatures between -20°C to -25°C accompanied soft, smooth snow conditions, highly favourable for travel. Sastrugi heights of 150 mm to 300 mm were manageable. The Kharkovchanka and sleds gouged trailing tracks 150 mm deep. Our only reason to grumble – extreme glare from ever-present sunshine. A late start meant a late finish to achieve the daily travel target of 70 km. We continued driving until 10:15pm. Today's menu comprised breakfast of potatoes, lunch of macaroni, and dinner of macaroni with fried chopped liver. To break the monotony, and probably because of the monotony, an argument erupted around the trivial issue of opening a can of milk.

Saturday 21 January 1984:

We camped at pole 300 ready to push on to GM13 the following day. For some reason Slava fell ill, an unusual event we attributed to a combination of altitude and exhaustion. Although, we also wondered whether dinner may have been responsible: a scrumptious combination of tinned sausage meat, herrings in tomato sauce, bread and butter, and marmalade. Slava wintered at Vostok the previous year, so altitude sickness seemed an implausible reason.

The weather continued fine and cold with ice haloes around the sun, a common indicator of fine weather. To date, our continual need to replace broken track pins was the most pressing issue to affect progress. But now we had a more serious development: the need to replace broken grouser plates. I listened to radio activity on 14 MHz and caught fragments of conversations between amateurs in the Pacific and US. I didn't attempt an outbound transmission due to continuing power issues in the Kharkovchanka.

Sunday 22 January 1984:

In a remarkable first, we completed a full day's travel of 70 km without sighting a single marker pole. GM13 is the intersection point between the Soviet Mirny to Dome C line and the Australian inland traverse route from Casey over which I travelled in 1978. The lack of route markers forced us to zigzag, a costly search process in time and wasted distance, plus it consumed a disproportionate volume of fuel. The Soviet pole line over this section supposedly consisted of alternating unpainted aluminium poles and wooden stakes – both difficult to pinpoint against an austere white landscape. My eyesight was excellent and I had experience spotting marker poles from my year at Casey, but I found the unpainted aluminium poles impossible to spot until we were within 200 m. We noticed several unmarked poles encountered in previous days had an upturned boot sitting on the top of the pole, confirming that we were not the first to experience difficulties finding the route markers.

Unfortunately, the Kharkovchanka parked 20 metres away from the ice movement marker, further than usual and too far for my liking. Connecting the JMR receiver to the antenna required two lengths of cable, and therefore a preamplifier to boost signal strength. After testing combinations of antenna leads and preamps, I discovered both preamplifiers were unserviceable. Deeply frustrated, my previous 'concern' escalated to panic regarding the growing list of failed equipment.

Monday 23 January 1984:

Despite exhaustion and another late night, I crawled out of my sleeping bag first thing in the morning to test the preamp. I hoped for a miracle and was disappointed. By the time we departed, I had one full cassette of data only. The poor strength of the received signal resulted in many missed satellite passes. Fortunately, GM13 was a low priority data station. I trudged 4 km around the accumulation polygon that surrounded the ice movement station. Slava joined me, both for safety and exercise. The sun shone brightly with a calm breeze of two knots. Perfect weather and very soft snow conditions were evidenced by 300 mm deep tracks gouged by prime movers on the way in. For no good reason, I created a gift parcel including a card for collection by the next passing group, likely to be Australians from Casey the following summer. I fastened it to the GM13 signpost with flimsy string, but never received contact from anyone who may have collected it. I assume it was never collected – probably swept away in a blizzard.

Tuesday 24 January 1984:

A monotonous day followed during which I experimented with JMR power arrangements. I continued to travel in the ATT and relied on Vlad to disconnect the battery charger inside the Kharkovchanka each time the vehicle stopped moving.

Entertainment devices I packed for the traverse included a state-of-the-art Sony Walkman and a dozen music CDs that I offered on loan to my colleagues. Several were enthusiastic and enjoyed the novelty of this new form of entertainment, passing it amongst themselves. On one occasion however, during a period of idle time while the mechanics were busy performing vehicle clutch repairs, one of our team came stomping over to me with my Walkman in hand. Scowling and without hesitating, he muttered, 'These tapes are crap … they're 10 years old.' That was all he said, then he turned and stomped off.

I wasn't sure whether the interaction was an attempt at a lame joke, or an insult, or sarcasm. I heard his words clearly. I observed his body language, but I was totally unsure how to interpret the message. At the time, Western rock music was popular in the USSR, but access to the latest music releases was limited. My colleagues knew the names of the popular bands (mostly American): Santana, Michael Jackson, David Bowie, Tears for Fears, U2, Spandau Ballet, The Police, Lionel Ritchie, R.E.M., The Pretenders, ELO, Kiss, Billy Joel, Toto, Hall and Oats, Cyndi Lauper, Men at Work, Bob Seger and the Silver Bullet Band, Kenny Rogers and Dolly Parton. The problem was, I was fixated on blues albums from the 1970s, not the top of the pops. In the eyes of (I'll call him X), 'What was the point of bringing the Walkman!'

This day I spoke to 'Jim' on Norfolk Island, then listened to a conversation involving an operator mobile at Halley Bay while I waited to connect with Earl. As I commenced, the batteries went flat. Not to worry, Kerry had not returned from Sydney. We rescheduled for two days later.

Wednesday 25 January 1984:

I slept until 9:15am while vehicle repairs continued. This particular breakdown involved an unserviceable clutch on the ATT and was serious enough to warrant, on completion, a toast of vodka and chocolates. We wasted no time moving away. Travel commenced at 5pm. I hoped to run the JMR overnight at the next station, GM19, but failed again to locate the ice movement station marker after missing five consecutive route markers.

Thursday 26 January 1984:

My rescheduled radio sked' turned into another missed opportunity due to lack of power. I could hear Kerry; she could not hear me.

The team vibe became crotchety, evidenced by a change in small routines and a noticeable increase in prickly behaviour. For some reason, the timing of lunch breaks had changed from 2pm to 1:30pm: a small adjustment, you'd think. But, at the time, this kind of issue had the potential to cause a raging argument. Our target arrival for Dome C was the end of January, only a few days away. We continued past GM25 without pause, travelling towards GM28 and camping overnight at pole marker 400, putting us 800 km out from Pionerskaya.

The prime movers strained under the load of continuing soft snow conditions, gouging 500 mm deep tracks and groaning under the weight of the trailing balok, which became both a grader and an anchor due to its low ground clearance. The belly of the van skidded directly on the surface in many sections, with sled runners dangling loose in the ruts. Occasionally the prime mover would spin in its tracks during a gear change or course adjustment, causing even deeper rutting. The heavier tow loads imposed by the additional drag further increased the risk of breaking tow chains and links.

Friday 27 January 1984:

We travelled non-stop to GM28 arriving at 3pm to establish camp. I powered up the JMR and set off alone to walk around the accumulation remeasurement polygon. Soft snow made the going difficult. Each step broke the crispy thin crust, with my feet sinking above the ankles like you would if crossing a silty mud-flat in concrete boots. Once the surface gave way, support disappeared.

While trudging around, suddenly and without warning the entire surface collapsed in an outward spiral. A booming, thunderous noise exploded, sounding something like a mixture of a thunderclap and the screaming roar of a jet fighter. I couldn't understand what had happened and it scared the living daylights out of me. The collapse of mere centimetres was clearly visible but I truly thought I was about to disappear in a crevasse. I froze. My heart rate exploded. Against all sensibilities I thought, *Crevasses ... no way ... impossible, not out here.* Logic didn't matter. I was so scared I couldn't think rationally. I could hear, see and follow the surreal, nerve-wracking sounds of the rumbling as the collapse spiralled outwards and away from me. The spirals (several of them) splintered, cracked and worked their way in criss-crossing patterns, hundreds of metres from the epicentre where I stood.

Huddled over a theodolite conducting a field magnetic measurement half a kilometre away, Vlad and Serge (magnetologist) heard the same noise and looked up. I, meanwhile, remained frozen to the spot, looking directly at them, terrified. They may not have appreciated my terror. After a few moments, they waved nonchalantly and I waved back to signal I was okay. The entire event lasted less than a minute, during which I stood absolutely still, utterly petrified. I had cracked a thin wind crust (like walking on thin ice) that overlay a honeycomb formation of subsurface ice crystals formed in a process called deposition, or desublimation, where ice crystals grow directly from water vapour then transform into solid ice without passing through a liquid phase. Overlying this thick layer of crystals was a smooth, brittle and very thin surface wind crust on which I had walked to trigger the collapse.

The weather was splendid, -17°C, not a breath of wind, and a low-hanging sun that illuminated our vehicles with an orange glow and super-long shadows.

Saturday 28 January 1984:

Only 14 km covered today before another serious mechanical breakdown to the ATT. Initial assessments suggested clutch issues. Closer inspection revealed a serious gearbox failure. Fortunately, the favourable weather (a balmy -7°C) allowed repairs to commence immediately.

Working on heavy machinery outdoors in the Antarctic is not pleasant at the best of times, our driver's gelid expression a clear indication of our collective mood. Sombre, pensive and emotive, they gushed slobbery saliva while working and talking, interspersed with dribbly spitting and mute periods of unsmiling contemplation. The sun blazed and circled high to our north in the morning, then by evening, low and speeding across the distant horizon. Long evening shadows became proportionally longer as bitter night temperatures descended. I climbed down from the Kharkovchanka at 6pm, by which time work had ceased. Inside the balok our team sipped a cuppa. Valery had evidently crushed his fingers and was being treated by the doctor. Two fingers on his left hand were bandaged, with blood seeping through. Our location at the time was near pole 427.

By 7:30pm the air temperature had dropped from a daytime high of -7°C to an evening low of -30°C. A dark grey stripe emerged on the horizon to the northeast, a sure sign of bad weather. By 9:30pm the dark grey stripe dominated the entire sky.

Sunday 29 January 1984:

With repairs complete before the approaching blizzard arrived, our travel day became a dash to the next overnight stop. We chipped off 60 km of hard-earned progress to reach pole 457. High altitude and deteriorating fitness had extracted a significant toll from us, affecting our capacity to perform physical tasks. Ultrasoft snow conditions continued. The balok and fuel sled both continued to toboggan on the underbelly of the superstructure, with ski runners 'hanging loose' in ruts gouged by the prime mover tracks.

Monday 30 January 1984:

Today's distance of approximately 70 km placed us at pole 490, approximately two to three days' travel from our Dome C destination. Mechanical problems continued. Another shattered track pin to the ATT crawler track was replaced without difficulty, but the repair consumed another valuable hour. I finished reading Gorky Park. On average, I read one novel per week then donated them to colleagues. Most books went straight to Vlad, although others took some, mostly to pass on as souvenirs to younger relatives back home.

Tuesday 31 January 1984:

Mechanical breakdowns took a turn for the worse with a fourth major incident. This time the ATT broke a track pin and rolled entirely off the right-hand crawler track. The repair consumed two worrisome hours while the guys in the Kharkovchanka continued on ahead, unaware of our predicament. Accordingly, the lunchtime rendezvous occurred hours later than usual. I counted 18 track pins replaced to date on the ATT. The number replaced on the Kharkovchanka would have been many times more.

Keen to maintain pace, we grabbed an informal lunch of bread and tinned fish and carried it to the vehicle to eat in the cab from our laps, an almost impossible feat. Generally speaking, we did not eat while moving. Normally we stopped, for both respite from cabin noise and respite from the shaking caused by rough terrain. If you tried to eat while moving and lifted hands away from your plate to hang on while crashing over sastrugi, food would always end up on the floor. And the floor was not clean!

Rather strange weather today, consisting of light snowfall and a blurry-looking sun moving across the horizon at a low declination*.

My feet felt unusually cold. I was fine when walking but uncomfortable when standing. In the evening, I discovered why after removing my boots. The insoles were completely frozen. The previous evening, I had not followed my usual practice of placing my boots upside down on the water heater to warm-up and thaw.

Incredibly, Slava reported a UFO sighting, which he described as a red-and-yellow disc that appeared in the sky for a short time and darted all over the place. No-one else saw it. We discussed his observation and apart from Slava himself, the remainder of us were sceptical. We agreed unanimously, however, that Slava was not the type of person to concoct a story. Slava was steadfast; he definitely saw a UFO. None of us observed any other UFOs during the traverse. The rest of us felt he more likely saw an illusion caused by sun, smoke, his eyes or his sunglasses. Perhaps it was a disintegrating meteorite. Prior to going to Casey in 1978 a geology professor advised me in earnest to look-out for remnants of meteorites on the inland ice surface.

Ongoing delays caused by breakdowns and maintenance limited our potential to achieve average daily travel goals, although today we advanced to GM22, 98 km from the Dome C camp. I operated the JMR overnight and retired to my bunk late in the evening after traipsing around another accumulation grid, followed by the collection of a snow sample. Dinner continued along a familiar theme – macaroni with meat and soup. Overnight temperatures dropped to around -30°C.

Wednesday 1 February 1984:

Our overnight stop at pole 555 positioned us even closer to Dome C camp, 1,110 km from Pionerskaya to be precise. Our travel plan discussed in previous days, involved no stops through to Dome C, so I was surprised when we pulled up. But then, during the day I had been in the cabin of the ATT, separate from the main team.

When I walked over to the Kharkovchanka to catch up on the latest plans, I discovered a raging argument in full swing about why and whether we should be stopping.

I cranked the amateur radio into action and established contact with the father of a high school friend who lived around the corner from my parents in North Balwyn. He alerted my parents at once, 'I've made contact with Trev!' My parents scurried around for a brief conversation. The signal was excellent initially but deteriorated quickly. I could barely hear them, although they seemed able to hear me.

Today's dinner broke the trend of macaroni. Chef Sergey served an innovative smorgasbord of canned pork, tuna, baked beans, hot porridge, bread and butter. I noticed also that our stores remained well stocked with nuts, chocolate, sweets and condiments from Mawson. The exterior air temperature of -41°C was probably 71°C lower than the interior. I couldn't breathe. My bed sheets and body were covered in sweat, my leg muscles sore, every air vent closed, our one and only thermometer off the scale – it maxed out at 21°C. I pleaded to open an air vent. Desperate, I jumped out of my bunk at 3am to throw open the exterior door, after which I felt comfortable enough to sleep. But my comfort didn't last. When I stepped into the Kharkovchanka at lunchtime all the air vents were closed again. Despite the physical readings appearing on the thermometer, I diarised again how the eerie stillness outside, combined with strong sunshine, seemed to disguise temperature. The thermometer recorded -41°C, but it simply didn't feel cold.

At Dome C, 1,500 km from Mirny

Thursday 2 and Friday 3 February 1984:
Drenched by intense sunshine, the morning travel commenced in blistering temperatures of -4°C, a big change from overnight minimums. Our arrival at Dome C camp coincided with a lunch stop at 1pm. The men rushed instinctively and single-mindedly

to US food dumps and started digging immediately, looking for items to augment our provisions. Meanwhile, I waited for Sergey (radio operator) to complete the official sked'. He seemed to take longer than usual, due, he said, to difficulties receiving messages in English from a new operator at Vostok! 'Messages in English?' I thought. This could only mean one thing: a telegram for me. Of course, it was from my darling wife Kerry – one of only two written messages I received during the entire period I was away.

Kerry prepared her telex based on impractical advice, using the ANARE teleprinter coding system known informally as a 'wyssa'* (pronounced whizzer). The wyssa – a system of five letter telegraphic codes developed by ANARE prior to the availability of satellite communications – required both the sender and the receiver to consult a code book.

The AAD publication *Communicating with Antarctica* was the wyssa bible. Code word phrases 'saved on wordage', it proclaimed. The wyssa encouraged expeditioners to achieve value-for-money from the free allocation limit of 200 telegraph codewords per month, the alternative being expensive charges for messages written in plain English that required far more characters. Those who exceeded the allocation limit could expect a debit charge on return to Australia of six cents per word.

First, you had to figure out what to say from the codes organised by subject index, an immensely time-consuming task made excruciating by attempts to personalise the phrases. WYSSA was a code word itself, that meant literally 'all my (our) love darling', not to be confused with a similar code 'WYZZA', which meant 'please don't wait so long next time'. Receiving a wyssa was equally mind-numbing. The thoughts and feelings people wished to share were not matters translated neatly into prescribed phrases or codes, even when garnished with adjectives, adverbs and a sprinkling of additional nouns.

I'm not sure exactly how Kerry's telegram made its way to me. Initially to Mawson, that's certain. At Mawson it must have been decoded into plain English then forwarded by telex in English to the Russian base at either Molodezhnaya or Mirny. From there, I suspect it was forwarded to the Russian station at Vostok (in Cyrillic characters probably mimicking the English alphabet) and finally to me via radio operators using morse code. The handwritten message I received was an incoherent scribbling on a scrap of paper, but the sentiment was obvious.

For the families of expeditioners at permanent Australian stations, sending a wyssa required the originator to mail a pre-coded message to 'Personal Cables, Antarctic Division', enclosing the sender's name and address. Alternatively, one could forward a telegram directly to an Antarctic station from a post office, with increased likelihood of it going to the wrong person or wrong base, and greater risk of a code being misspelled. A wyssa sent from AAD Head Office radio room was received by telex printout in the radio room of the applicable Antarctic station. The uncoded message was handed to the receiver who translated it back into English using the 'Decode' section of his or her personal hardcopy of the *Communicating with Antarctica* book. Codewords were structured into subject matter groups such as Missing You, Misunderstanding, Morale, Mother, Mother's Day, New Year, No, Penguin and so on. A separate Decode section listed the codewords in alphabetic order.

The process seemed straightforward until you tried it. A translation error could easily, and did, cause confusion. Consider the following exaggerated example: 'YIHPY YARAJ WYMMA YINAP WYVWE' which means: 'Hello and how are you? Have met with an accident. Please don't worry. The food is first rate and I've put on some weight. Best love for our anniversary.' Suppose the message was mistyped or transcribed as, 'YINPA YARJA WYNNA YINAC WYWYE'. The codes look similar but now mean: 'Glad to hear. Injury is not serious. Hope you will soon be better. Did not hear your message on Radio Australia. Merry Christmas and Happy New Year.'

The codebook offered many sections for unique Antarctic topics, some with limited appeal for family and friends in Australia. On the topic of beards (as in facial hair), several choices were available: YIGUM, YIHKE, YIHMO and YIJNO. YIHMO offered outstanding value for money: 'I've grown a beard, but I think I'll shave it off before I get back to Australia.' That's 13 real words for just six cents! Another code offered great value plus humour at no extra cost, but could only be used by Mawsonites – YITUB: 'I am not sure whether men training dogs or dogs training men.' LOL. The codebook offered three choices under the heading No[9]; YAAWN, YALOG and YOOZK.

By today's standards, messages to Antarctica were costly. Repeated transmissions of long teletype messages could slash an expeditioner's savings. Hence, family members were sometimes overcautious, exemplified by the codes YONAT (Can afford longer messages) and YAAHY (Longing to hear from you again darling). The whole process was sterile and hard to imagine in today's world in which everyone has a smart phone and texting has replaced phone calls as a primary means of communication.

After I returned to Australia, Kerry explained her feelings as an 'Antarctic wife', particularly the way lack of communication with me affected her ... deeply. Whereas families of expeditioners at Australian stations were well supported by the Antarctic Wives network, I was not at an Australian base. The support network did not work for Kerry during my Soviet experience. It added to, rather than eased, her stress. During my absence, Kerry was offered occasional advice: 'This is not what marriage is about!'

---

9. Look them up yourself!

Kerry also felt vulnerable at home, given our house was family-sized, open plan and set on a heavily treed block. We were lucky to have understanding neighbours in case of emergency. Kerry often sat up until 2am watching the 1984 Sarajevo Winter Olympics, and several times men in brown suits, literally men dressed in brown suits who Kerry assumed to be private detectives, came knocking on the door during the early hours, ostensibly chasing debts from a previous occupant. Adding to her feelings of insecurity, Kerry believed our landline was bugged. To an Australian this sounds farfetched. Suggest the same to a Russian and the response will be very different, most likely an immediate nodding head. At times, irregular and obvious clicking sounds occurred when Kerry answered the phone – alerting her in a manner similar to the pause we hear today that warns of an unsolicited marketing call. The clicking was not evident prior to my departure, nor was it apparent after I returned. But consider reality for a moment: I was on a Soviet expedition … with a diplomatic passport … during a particularly sensitive period of the Cold War.

Kerry was unaware of my exact location during most of my absence. Obviously, she knew I was in Antarctica, but that was all. Always on edge and fearful for my safety, her confidence was shaken one day when a work colleague of mine rang to enquire where I was. It was around the time of our arrival at Dome C. 'Hi,' he said, 'we were just wondering whether you know of Trevor's whereabouts … exactly?' Kerry replied politely, 'Well, no! I was hoping you could tell me!' I tried, but was unable to speak to Kerry while at Dome C. And wouldn't you know it, propagation conditions were perfect! I talked to Earl who taped our conversation, presumably to play back later for Kerry, but she was distressed and not interested in details of my exploits. She just wanted to hear my voice.

For those of us directly involved, arrival at Dome C camp (74° 44'S, 124° 22'SE, 3,213 m above sea level) was incredibly exciting.

The gruelling 1,500 km over-snow traverse from Mirny was a massive achievement irrespective of how many parties had succeeded before us. Dome C camp was a significant geographic location visited by few human beings at the time. Unmanned, it functioned as a casual base for US summer science activities. The weather was okay but not great. Daytime temperatures hovered around -36°C, the wind slightly breezy.

We exhumed a half-buried doorway into what appeared to be the main building, a canvas-clad Nissen hut. Venturing inside, we found a note sitting loosely but prominently on top of a dining table directly in front of the entrance. The note was dated and placed there by the Americans who flew in from McMurdo three weeks earlier for maintenance on the automatic weather station. We also found four boxes of materials from a visiting Russian scientist working at the time at South Pole station. The note requested delivery of all four boxes back to Leningrad – a bizarre and surprising discovery that Vlad did not expect. Obviously, leaving boxes for us to collect was premeditated by individuals who knew about our traverse, but it seemed unusual and risky given no-one had communicated with us beforehand.

We entered several other buildings, one of them a small orange fibreglass building visible miles away, the 'Glaciology Hut'. I left my business card (Trevor Hamley – Glaciologist) sitting on the table hoping to prompt contact from someone/anyone at a later date, but I never received a follow-up. Perhaps I should have left a note saying, 'Please call me, whoever you are.' As far as I know, Vlad also did not receive a response to the numerous queries he issued by telegram beforehand inquiring about possible US visits to Dome C, yet evidence of a visit was everywhere. Apart from the four boxes of papers from South Pole station that we discovered by chance, the most significant physical evidence were fresh tracks on the ski way. During the traverse to date, I had sent numerous unanswered telegrams via

Sergey (radio operator) requesting a radio sked' with colleagues in Australia and at Australian Antarctic stations. I suspect my messages were lost in translation, or delayed by transmission difficulties, or simply not answered. Having explored the buildings and satisfied our curiosity, we pulled up stakes and headed a few kilometres beyond the Dome C station to establish a new ARMS and then rest following six weeks of continuous, exhausting travel. An astonishing shimmer of mirages surrounded us on the horizon during the early evening.

Saturday 4 February 1984:

Our main activity for the day was to gather for a group photo, or series of photos dressed in light clothing, with the daytime temperature registering -35°C

Sunday 5 February 1984:

Maintenance complications with the ARMS forced a longer stay at GM29 (Dome C). Overnight minimums were sinking to -45°C, imposing significant constraints on outdoor pursuits.

I used the extra time to fiddle with my equipment, including a further attempt to fix a problem with the radio antenna. The JMR continued operating without dramas and filled three cassettes with satellite doppler data, more than sufficient for an accurate position fix. I also uncovered the cause of my problems with the Astro C antenna tuner – two internal rubber drive belts frozen solid. It seemed they would remain flexible only in temperatures above -20°C. If the tuner remained outside at lower temperatures, I risked them breaking from brittle fracture, and I did not have spares. I briefly considered but did not pursue the idea of asking Valentine to build a heating circuit. Mainly because our vehicle power supply was unreliable and limited. Instead, after experimenting with wiring configurations I found an improved position for the tuner inside the van, in a vacant location intended for navigation equipment and not used during our traverse.

After repositioning the tuner, I put out a CQ call and received a response from an Australian teacher in Botswana named Don. Our conversation evolved naturally into questions about where each of us lived, where we were raised, and where we went to school. Amazing coincidences followed. Don revealed his previous teaching positions were Monterey Technical College in Frankston, and Toorak College in Mt Eliza. Incredibly, Kerry was teaching at Monterey High School at the time, located only kilometres from the Tech', and Toorak College was only two kilometres from our home in Mt Eliza. Unfortunately, Kerry wasn't involved in the conversation. I believe she may have had a school commitment or school function, or perhaps was at a year level camp, or maybe just asleep at home. It was 1100am GMT or 10:00pm AEST. After the conversation finished, I received a call from Mawson, who reported my signal was 'booming in'.

Eventually the time came. We pulled up stumps and commenced our return trek. We had a new straw broom and exciting new ingredients including tomato juice, tinned ravioli, frankfurters and sultanas. We lived high on the hog for the next week or two.

Kerry feared I may never return as I walked down the gangplank to board Nella Dan

At Mawson. My gear filled the tray of a small Utility Truck

The Ilyushin 14 parked on sea ice in Kista Strait, Mawson

*The Mirny OIC (front left seat) and IL14 Pilot (rear right seat)
arrive at Mawson*

A photo opportunity during our tour of Mawson

Snoopy is introduced to the Mirny OIC and new owner

The burnt out remains of the Vostok powerhouse with ice-core drilling tower in the background

Drinks with the Vostok Officer in Charge

The ATT Tractor Train

The Kharkovchanka Tractor Train at an ice movement station

Vlad undertaking an absolute magnetic measurement

Installing an Automatic Remote Magnetic Station (ARMS)

Trevor and Vlad at the GM13 Drum Beacon –
where Soviet and Australian Traverse lines cross

Reinstating an unravelled crawler track

The look of cold

Hammering track pins – a tiresome and frequent task

Hammering track pins while lying on your back was utterly exhausting

Doctor Slava preparing cracked pepper

Preparing Christmas dinner

New Years Eve party inside the balok

Removing a gearbox outside at minus forty is not fun

Vlad holds a loose screw found inside the JMR.
Astro C pictured behind him

Treeva Kalinitch models vallinke, shapka and Russian padded trousers

At Dome C. A group photo minus Vlad, who was the photographer

The IL14 on approach for an airdrop

The IL14 made several passes at GM28, just after the appendicectomy

An Emergency

SOVIET UNION
ILLUSTRATED MONTHLY

No. 7 (424) 1985

Founded by Maxim Gorky in 1930 as USSR IN CONSTRUCTION. Renamed in 1950
Published in Arabic, Bengali, Chinese, English, Finnish, French, German,
Hindi, Hungarian, Italian, Japanese, Korean, Mongolian, Portuguese,
Rumanian, Russian, Serbo-Croat, Spanish, Urdu, and Vietnamese

FORCED DECISION—MAKING

Their sledge trip was in its second month. All this time their living space was confined to a tractor with a wooden trailer house and the Kharkovchanka cross-country vehicle. Outside there was a ringing 60° C frost and a lifeless expanse of snow all around.

Nine members of the Antarctic expedition from the polar geomagnetic research laboratory of the Institute of Terrestrial Magnetism, the Ionosphere and Radio Wave Propagation, the USSR Academy of Sciences, were returning from dome "S" situated at an altitude of over 3,000 metres above sea level near the south geomagnetic pole. Surgeon Vyacheslav Mogirev from Moscow had been appointed doctor of the expedition. Before that, he had wintered at Vostok, the least accessible station on the continent, where minus 80° C temperatures are usual.

They were 1,215 kilometres from the Mirny observatory when the party's leader Vladimir Papitashvili ordered a halt for carrying out routine scientific work.

After the trip in the rumbling vehicle, Mogirev was having a rest in the cosy quiet of the small sleigh-house when engineer Valentin Gorbachev approached him.

"Something's wrong with me, doc," he said. "I thought it'd pass, but the pain keeps getting worse."

Mogirev was quick to diagnose appendicitis. He also realised that he had an emergency situation on his hands and that an immediate operation was imperative. Papitashvili radioed to Mirny and received instructions: prepare a landing strip. The time factor was all that mattered then.

The patient's condition was rapidly going from bad to worse. The drugs were no longer of any use, and Valentin could hardly repress the fierce pain.

Frozen and all in hoar-frost, Papitashvili reported from the threshold: "Lousy snow, all crumbly. You can't compact it." It became clear that they could not rely on the aircraft. So the surgeon decided to operate.

They thoroughly washed the floor and the walls with acetous boiling water and partitioned off the beds with sterile sheets. The dinner table became a makeshift operating table. The diesel stove was switched off to avoid soot. Papitashvili and the driver, Sergei Yakovlev, were to assist Mogirev, and the radio operator, Sergei Zamyashlyaev, was to maintain constant contact with Mirny.

The temperature in the sleigh-house was falling, but they were unaware of the cold. Dressed in thin woollen underwear, in sterile overalls, they spent two long hours at the table. Hardly had he made the incision than Mogirev realised the timeliness of the operation: it was suppurative appendicitis.

Two days later the tractor and Kharkovchanka started off. In another month they were welcomed at Mirny. Gorbachev's condition was excellent.

At present, Vyacheslav Mogirev is back at his Moscow hospital and often reminisces about the Antarctic where his former patient has returned on another expedition.

S. SNEGIREV

Surgeon Vyacheslav Mogirev and his assistant, the party's chief Vladimir Papitashvili

Photographs by M. NACHINKIN and V. PAPITASHVILI

A 1985 newsclip from the 'Soviet Union Illustrated Monthly'

The ATT bogged again with a broken crawler track

*The Kharkovchanka tows the ATT back onto its broken crawler
track to effect repairs*

QSL cards waiting for me in Australia

Reunion with the Vostok crew at Pionerskaya

On the outskirts of Mirny, we stop as the IL14 swoops during another flight to Molodezhnaya

At Mirny. The view from Dom Geophysik looking upslope to Dom Radio

At Mirny. The view from Dom Radio looking downslope to Dom Geophysik

Mirny Departure Day. Personal bags loaded, we are about to scramble in

Being hoisted aboard the Kapitan Gotsky

The Kapitan Gotsky lounge area

The Baikal follows the Kapitan Gotsky through the sea ice

Onboard the Baikal, dancing girls with a four piece band.
A great way to travel home

CHAPTER 5

Return to Base

YAHOC WYTOY YASKA

Had a party last night to celebrate. I think about you all the time and hope you are getting along all right. It has been very cold.

Good News and Bad News

Monday 6 February 1984:

Return to Mirny was underway. But first an ARMS installation beckoned at pole 565, 10 km to the west of Dome C camp – a location slightly closer to the South Geomagnetic Pole. Ignoring further difficulties, we anticipated one day at the new location: sufficient for a position fix using the JMR.

Tuesday 7 February 1984:

Amateur radio was entertaining, but frequently scratchy and inconsistent. Unable to contact Earl initially, I dropped into a conversation between Ron at Casey and a mechanic named Mikhail based at Vostok.

Earl chimed in to suggest we change frequencies to avoid competing with other users on the same band. Arrangements became complicated. Vostok-based Mikhail was listening to Earl, me and a Japanese ham radio operator. My parents' neighbour in Melbourne was also listening. Call signs started to crossover. To confuse matters, a new operator named John from Perth – who I didn't know previously – came booming in to introduce himself. Like fishing, you never knew who you might hook up with. If you were lucky, you might even contact the person you wanted to contact. Over dinner we adjusted clocks to synchronise with Mirny at seven hours ahead of GMT. The weather remained fine. Temperatures were still in the minus 30s. Vlad and Valery both reported feeling tight in the chest. They retired early and spent much of the following day resting.

> *Wednesday 8 February 1984:*
>
> *I slept badly last night, too hot and sweaty in the sauna-like conditions. I hopped up early, dressed and tried to read while sitting on the step of the external doorway with the door ajar. The overnight camp at GM22 allowed an 1100 GMT sked' with my supervisor to update progress and discuss JMR issues. Constant interjection from strangers wanting to exchange QSL cards frustrated coherent discussion.*

> *Thursday 9 February 1984:*
>
> *I had enough passes collected by midday to complete the position measurement. The team continued replacing track pins, a daily task now of equal importance to checking engine oil and antifreeze. Vlad immersed himself preparing telegrams to plead for more track pins. Our meagre stocks were almost exhausted. On any given day we normally replaced several track pins. Today we replaced 30 on the Kharkovchanka alone. The mammoth task consumed half a day of hard labour for several men.*

I managed a rare opportunity to talk to Kerry in a sked' before departure. I was over the moon to simply hear her voice. Earl also passed on exciting world news. On 8 February three Soviet cosmonauts launched on a space mission to visit the Soviet space station Salyut 7. Tasked to perform maintenance, the crew used flashlights to enter the darkened station, which hadn't been visited for two years. They reactivated the station before settling into a routine of household chores and science experiments (sounds like us), ultimately setting a record for spacewalk hours. Earl also relayed news of a second US Challenger space shuttle mission launched on 3 February, the first to attempt an untethered spacewalk. For the first time, I picked up the AM signal of Radio Australia using the Astro C. Starved of information and news from the outside world for almost seven weeks, we listened keenly. 'Old Dedooshka', the official radio, couldn't receive AM signals. Having identified Radio Australia, we then scanned for Radio Moscow and tuned in regularly. Next, more out of curiosity than anything else, we searched for and found the Voice of America. A new entertainment routine was born!

Now that half our fuel had been consumed, we had lighter tow loads and a faster average travel speed. Lighter tow loads combined with less frequent stops enabled more ambitious travel targets. Our new target became 100 km per day. We aimed to reach sequential ice movement stations one hop at a time.

Friday 10 February 1984:

We arrived at GM21 at 7am completely exhausted. I set up and started the JMR. By the time I'd finished my companions were fast asleep. Like a naughty child I relished my free access to the kitchen where I prepared a light breakfast of coffee and porridge.

Yesterday's success tuning-in to Radio Australia prompted a listening watch at every opportunity. At the very next news bulletin, Radio Australia floored us with an astonishing announcement, 'Radio Moscow is playing sombre music in place of its normal light music program,' pointing to the passing of a prominent Kremlin official. My shocked companions wondered why no similar information was yet circulating from Soviet Antarctic stations. We immediately searched for confirmation from Radio Moscow. Indeed, normal broadcasts had ceased. Sombre music played endlessly, which also reflected our mood. Our team was starting to crack at the edges from fatigue, boredom and the monotony of our daily routine. The increasing number of vehicle breakdowns added significant stress. I worried we might be forced to abandon the science program and run for home before completing the remeasurement of outstanding ice movement stations. According to our sometimes functional 'minimum temperature' thermometer, overnight temperatures were regularly dipping to -55°C.

Saturday 11 February 1984:

Verbal announcements on both the English and Russian service of Radio Moscow confirmed yesterday's sombre music. Yuri Andropov had passed away.

Yuri Andropov, General Secretary of the Communist Party and successor to Leonid Brezhnev, spent a short but significant 15-month period as leader of the Soviet party, following an unusually long 15-year reign as Chairman of the KGB. Although only in power for a short time, Andropov left a huge legacy. He brought to the fore a new generation of reform-minded leaders including Mikhail Gorbachev. My companions speculated, 'All eyes across the Soviet Union will focus now on who might lead the funeral commissary' – this being the unspoken indication of the new leader. Radio Moscow broadcasts were faint and indistinct, but we glued ears to the radio for updates. Andropov's passing created a convenient distraction from our own concerns, including the desperate shortage of track pins. Incoming telegrams regarding our request for an airdrop were non-committal. We speculated that Serdyukov may feel conflicted by the disruption our demands placed on crucial Vostok resupply flights.

Commenting on the death of Yuri Andropov, Vlad referred to the 'funn-eyral'. I couldn't understand what he thought was funny. Similarly, he couldn't understand why I looked perplexed. He reached for the dictionary and scrambled through the pages before pointing to the word … 'funeral'. Ooh! And the penny dropped.

'Lunch' occurred at 6pm, a major departure in routine and thus a significant event. The overnight temperature plunged to -56.5°C. Seriously cold!

Field Appendicectomy

Sunday 12 February 1984:

Sergey (radio operator) reorganised the official sked' with Vostok and Mirny to a timeslot two hours later than usual. We would now be mobile at times I had pre-arranged for radio contact with Australia. Nevertheless, I made three successful contacts: one with Casey and two with Mawson. I was unable to get through to Australia. We travelled to pole 420 at station GM28 (73° 52'S, 115° 07'E), located 300 km to the west of Dome C and 1,200 km from Mirny. Late in the day I became aware of Valentine G's visit to Doctor Slava during the morning, to complain of a sore tummy, followed by Slava's almost immediate diagnosis of appendicitis. Suddenly, shockingly, we plunged headlong into a medical nightmare. Every action refocussed immediately on saving Valentine's life. A sprint to Mirny required two weeks minimum non-stop, not allowing for breakdowns – too long.

Removing an appendix in a hospital may be routine and relatively low risk. Removing an appendix in a field caravan, high on the plateau of the Antarctic Ice Sheet, is life-threatening. Slava said he 'wasn't sure whether surgery was required'. I'm not sure anyone believed him. Although a practising abdominal surgeon in Moscow and the ideal specialist, he lacked trained assistants, theatre equipment and facilities. We had sufficient surgery-qualified linen, but only the barest range of surgical instruments and medicines. A general anaesthetic was out of the question. To the best of my knowledge, we had no blood products.

We gathered to discuss our situation. Slava remained with Valentine G to monitor his condition and discuss a likely course of events and options. I suggested, 'Perhaps we contact the Americans and request air evacuation by ski-equipped Hercules?' – an impractical idea, actually. Slava had no time to consult or reflect. While hoping to avoid an operation, he could not risk delaying preparations. At this stage he mostly worked alone, making repeated trips between the balok and the Kharkovchanka, chain-smoking throughout. He consolidated surgical equipment, consumables and instruments from various storage locations, identifying shortages along the way. His grim facial demeanour and trembling hands reflected considerable stress. Slava nominated and briefed two assistants – Vlad and Sergey (mechanic), both untrained. We all worried about the possible consequences of the surgery proceeding: a not insignificant matter.

Planning and organising a makeshift 'operating theatre' also commenced immediately. We had two less-than-ideal choices: either the wooden dining table in the balok, or a sturdier but very small metal table in the Kharkovchanka. Slava chose the balok, mainly due to superior natural light and space. Floors and walls were immediately scrubbed clean with boiled water. The diesel stove/heater was shut down to reduce the risk of contamination from airborne soot. We covered the dining table with white linen to reduce infection risk and improve reflected light. Improvised ward curtains were strung using white bedlinen.

Slava kept us informed. Valentine was stoic. He shed tears in private moments and was totally aware of the risks and possible outcomes. Sergey (radio operator) spent four hours tapping on the morse key in abysmal propagation conditions, attempting to break through to Soviet stations at either Mirny, Vostok or Molodezhnaya. Eventually he contacted Mirny which triggered a tidal wave response. Messages flowed back and forth in rapid succession for hours afterwards.

Vlad discussed our predicament with Mirny by radio, who requested we start levelling and compressing a 30 m wide by 200 m long runway, capable of receiving the IL14. However, the local soft snow surface made landing and take-off impossible for the IL14, and presumably also for a Hercules. We also knew (from previously aborted airdrops) an aircraft might struggle to find us under a heavy blanket of ground drift. Landing considerations aside, the patient's condition combined with the lead time for evacuation, made air repatriation untenable.

Monday 13 February 1984:

Monday the 13th is the Soviet equivalent of our Friday the 13th, a day to remember! I slept from 4am till 11am with one inter-ruption at 10am caused by the transmission of a synoptic weather report to Mirny. Valentine G's overnight condition remained stable but had not improved. Most importantly though, it hadn't deteriorated. Slava believed it too early to know whether an operation might be avoided. We didn't have long to wait. Next thing Vlad burst through the door, his tone forceful and serious. The operation would definitely proceed but the timing remained uncertain.

The afternoon passed in idle conversation. Time dragged. I read and listened to music. In the hours before the operation we limited numbers entering the balok to minimise disturbance to Valentine. Signs of action occurred at 5pm. Apart from Valentine and Slava, the rest of us had moved to the Kharkovchanka. Unable to read for sustained periods and too listless to work productively, I at least felt reassured by the throbbing hum of the generator – a bit like the comforting rhythms of a washing machine. I looked out the window and noticed something odd; the balok generator was also operating again. Seconds later we heard someone stomping around on the roof of the Kharkovchanka rummaging through crates and boxes. Then the interior door crashed open. Slava burst in, half-dressed, quietly uttering obscenities as he emptied cupboards and drawers, obviously searching for medical consumables. He stuffed various items (mostly bandages) into the pockets of his parka, then hurried outside, straight into temperatures in the minus 50s, which I'm damn sure he didn't even notice.

Despite the adverse weather and lack of an airdrop, Valentine's increasing body temperature persuaded Slava to proceed. Only the doctor, patient and the two surgery assistants occupied the theatre area of the balok from that point on. One person stood in the vestibule to act as a messenger. Valery monitored the balok generator without entering the theatre area. Continuous power supply and light were, of course, essential. Sergey (radio operator) manned the radio (again inside the balok but in a separate room), on constant standby.

Valentine G was a tough bugger. Immediately after the diagnosis we seriously discussed filling him with vodka and shoving a piece of timber in his mouth to bite due to the unavailability of a general anaesthetic. The two-hour surgery began with a local anaesthetic, performed under the light of two incandescent bulbs and two hand-held flashlights. Before making the first incision, Slava apparently turned to Vlad and asked, 'How do you feel about blood?' to which Vlad replied 'I'm okay, Doc' but he wasn't sure. He took several deep breaths to steady himself.

Locating Valentine's appendix proved difficult. It was tucked up the back near his spine, apparently not uncommon. Sergey (mechanic) held both flashlights and pointed them as directed. One was my Eveready Dolphin, the other belonged to Valentine himself. Vlad held Valentine's wound open using two surgical hooks. Valentine was alert and fully aware of what was happening. He swore profusely throughout the operation although not in pain.

A little later into the operation, Slava directed his assistants to adjust their position. Each assistant held a flashlight in one hand and used the other hand to hold a clamp. Slava eventually emerged from the balok at 11pm, reluctant to declare the operation a success, and worried about possible infection. Both doctor and patient prepared psychologically for a second procedure. Both expected complications. At the time, I was unaware of many details of the operation.

I carried on playing with my JMRs in the Kharkovchanka while the operation progressed in the balok. When I switched on the JMR and set it to standby, I noticed the clock would stop and not reset. I studied the manual. I stared at the machine hoping for inspiration. I tried turning things on and off. Nothing changed. Given the circumstances and likelihood of being stationary for some time, I disconnected the antenna and let the machine run while I mulled over possible remedies. We sat up all night waiting for the arrival of the IL14. Next morning, voila, I found the JMR working correctly.

Drained and exhausted, the stress of our situation exacted a toll on everyone, not just the patient and doctor. Incredibly, this was Slava's third appendix operation. The first was a serious case of peritonitis performed at Mirny before Slava flew to Vostok to winter through 1983. The second was conducted at Vostok itself, only the third since the station was established 34 years earlier in 1959. This operation on Valentine G, the third for Slava, was his first in the field and, as far as I am aware, the only field appendicectomy ever conducted in the history of Antarctic exploration. It was and still is unusual for a doctor to perform one appendicectomy in Antarctica, let alone three during a single tour of duty.

On a related matter, the requirement for all Antarctic expeditioners to have their appendix removed is a widespread and common misconception. ANARE, for example, requires only doctors to have their appendices removed. It is not a requirement for other expeditioners, nor is it for Soviet expeditions. The requirement came about for Australian expeditions after a disaster at Heard Island in 1950. The one and only doctor developed symptoms of appendicitis and prepared to operate on himself, but only went as far as marking his stomach! Eventually, the Navy returned this man to Australia in a highly expensive and unnecessary rescue that created front page news around Australia. *The Sydney Morning Herald* front page of Saturday 22 July 1950 headlined with 'Doctor to Remove His Own Appendix'. A frenzy of subsequently aborted private rescue missions preceded involvement by the Australian Navy. On arrival in Australia, the doctor walked ashore unaided, apparently recovered. Since then, ANARE have required all doctors to have their appendix removed. Slava's operation on Valentine G was even more dramatic and serious. In our eyes, it was equivalent to the legendary circumstances of 27-year-old Soviet doctor Leonid Rogosov (refer to Related Essay A – The Story of Leonid Rogosov) who famously removed his own appendix at Novolazarevskaya station in April 1961.

We received continuous updates from Mirny. Initially, poor weather prevented aircraft departure. Later, breaking conditions allowed the aircraft to take off at 10pm. The predicted ETA was three hours later, at around 1am. I provided position coordinates, including elevation and snow density in case of an unexpected landing. Sergey borrowed my 'long wire' antenna to establish a non-directional radio navigation beacon.

Tuesday 14 February 1984:

At 5am Valery and Sergey (cook/magnetologist) tramped off to make a smoke beacon by setting fire to diesel-soaked rags. The rags burned but produced putrid smoke that dribbled along the surface, driven by the slight breeze and trapped by the weight of the cold air mass above. Instead of generating a rising plume, the smoke eventually dispersed into ground-level haze to impede vision, not only at ground level, but also from above.

At 1am, the plane appeared on the horizon as predicted. A hefty vapour trail streamed behind, making it easy for us to spot against the glowing backlight of the apricot sky. The IL14 buzzed past at low altitude on the first of four loops, the rear door open and ready for action. The familiar engine roar was music to our ears. We waved energetically, as you'd imagine. Such an electric moment – the cockpit crew visible to us, bunched together and looking down inquisitively as they zoomed past. As the aircraft looped around for a second pass, all of us sprinted to the east as fast as we could in our heavy boots, stumbling and tripping over sastrugi to find a suitable position for a photograph.

On the second, third and fourth pass the aircraft flew close to stall speed with its nose raised, just 10 m above the surface. Long shadows heightened the drama. With each pass, one crate of track pins (for a total of three) came tumbling out of the rear door without a parachute. Several smaller, padded packages of medical supplies also tumbled out. Although we could not ignore the reason for the airdrop, including the substantial risks taken by the aircrew and aircraft itself, we were thrilled to witness an unforgettable, spine-tingling spectacle of raw adventure.

The crates of track pins were extremely heavy and exploded like bombs on impact with the surface, causing deep hollows. Steel pins and timber shards spewed in all directions. The crates themselves practically vapourised. Thanks to their thick padding and light weight, the smaller, lighter packages of medical supplies fared better. These bounced when they hit the surface, then skimmed along like bounce bombs from *The Dam Busters*. Inside, we found antibiotics, bottled oxygen, pharmaceuticals and, most importantly for others, four cartons of cigarettes (not the 10 cartons requested). Both doctor and patient slept soundly through the drama of the 15-minute air show. The aircraft carved away after the fourth pass, its wings waggling characteristically as it gathered momentum and altitude for the return leg. We spread out instinctively to recover the medical supplies, leaving the track pins where they lay for collection the following day.

Adding to our woes, Serge's radio transmitter stopped working. He spent one hour fiddling with knobs and dials, probing anxiously into the guts of the electricals before successfully returning the old girl to service. Sergey (mechanic) stayed with Valentine G while he slept-off the post-operation drowsiness. The rest of us slept soundly from 7am till 2pm, huddled in the Kharkovchanka. Valentine was talkative soon after the operation. He seemed in minor discomfort, but otherwise okay. The balok felt less like an operating theatre after removing the white sheets. The dining table remained cluttered with surgical equipment and drugs. Supplies from the airdrop remained ready at a moment's notice should Valentine's condition deteriorate. A lingering high temperature (38°C) warned of possible infection. During the evening, Slava prepared a written account of the operation. Vlad busied himself reviewing the field operation manual for guidance on who to inform, how and when, and clues about how to handle the situation officially. Fortunately, the weather remained fine and sunny, although damn cold. Daytime temperatures varied between -30°C to -38°C. Evening temperatures dropped below -50°C – the temperature was exactly -53°C when the IL14 arrived. Over dinner, I was chuffed by an unexpected compliment. Apparently, my Russian had 'improved'.

Wednesday 15 February 1984:

I climbed out of the bunk during the night to check the JMR and found the data cassette full. I disconnected the antenna, returned to my bunk and slept soundly until 10:30am. After rising again, I opened the JMR. Again, I stared numbly at the circuit boards before concluding, 'I can't do anything about these intermittent malfunctions. Who am I kidding?' I reassembled and warmed the JMR to make it ready for further operations. We spent most of the afternoon passing time idly. At 6pm the temperature started to drop. Without notice, Vlad and Valery (oddly I thought) went out to collect track pins, then commenced repairing the crawler tracks. A telegram arrived from Mirny suggesting we grade a landing strip by driving the Kharkovchanka up and down to level the sastrugi, a suggestion not received well by our team. Our stocks of diesel could not be wasted on such a risky evacuation strategy. The Kharkovchanka was more likely to mulch the surface than level it.

Dr Slava remained pensive and unsmiling. Although two days since the operation, the outcome was still in the balance. Valentine G was intermittently teary, when out of nowhere he declared, 'We will be getting underway tomorrow!' Something was obviously afoot. I wondered whether Valentine's brave face masked a deteriorating medical condition, a possibility no-one wanted. Slava revealed later that he was very concerned at the time about the likelihood of a second operation to address the enduring infection. Valentine joined us for dinner, sitting up with good face colour, but his body temperature stayed high.

Our dinner table remained set as a working operating theatre, cluttered with medical supplies: bandages, needles, syringes, drugs, a stethoscope, intravenous drips … and the most essential consumable, vodka. While the table remained in service for medical reasons, we ate meals standing in the kitchen or crouched in the corridor, typically taking food with a fork directly from a frying pan, or from a plate balanced on our knees.

Thursday 16 February 1984:

No-one stirred until midday. Afternoon activities involved the usual crawler track pin replacements and routine maintenance to prime movers. A new travel plan emerged to provide the least discomfort for Valentine G. We would retrace our tracks exactly, keeping sled runners within the snow-filled ruts generated on our outbound journey. Slava and Vlad would accompany Valentine in the Kharkovchanka. I would transfer to a bunk in the balok. Despite current circumstances, my focus remained on the science program. I wasn't uncaring – it was the best way to avoid becoming a burden. A telegram arrived from Australia suggesting I remove the DC power converter from JMR-4 and attach it to the outside of JMR-1 to facilitate the use of an antenna preamplifier. I mulled over the advantages and disadvantages, concerned whether I had sufficient time to complete the modifications before vehicle maintenance concluded. I decided to proceed but installed the converter inside, rather than outside JMR-1. Right in the middle of these repairs the mechanics advised both vehicles were ready to depart. Damn! I pleaded for an extra hour for testing. Understandably, Vlad and Valery were not happy, but agreed. I assessed the JMR's operation at the next available satellite pass. Straight away the JMR locked on to both display and standby mode with excellent signal strength. Phew! We could go.

The small delay I caused was subsequently diluted by a time-consuming process to transfer Valentine G from the balok back to the Kharkovchanka. The patient transfer required an exchange of bedding, plus the relocation of personal clothing and effects, including most of the medical consumables. Eventually, we moved away at 9pm, rattling along at a slow, steady pace before stopping for coffee at midnight, with 60 km covered. I dozed spasmodically as we travelled.

Friday 17 February 1984:

We arrived at our target destination GM25 by 7am. The Kharkovchanka parked in the path of outbound tracks as planned but, unfortunately for me, 14 m from the ice movement marker. The extended cable run to the pole-mounted antenna required the use of a preamplifier. I set about unpacking the JMR while creeping around the cabin (quiet as a mouse), while all others slept. I then slept from 9am to 1pm. Valentine's medical emergency obviously threatened the science program. It also changed our eating

*habits and diet, which became a revolving combination of bread
and jam, tinned fish and various canned foods.*

Days and nights became increasingly cold, forcing us to don more
layers of clothing. I now wore a woollen balaclava routinely under
my *shapka** to provide additional wind protection and neck warmth.

Saturday 18 February 1984:

*'Kak tee!' (what is one to do?) I couldn't sleep because of con-
stant sniffing. I felt I could not or should not complain, although
I threw out hints from time to time. It drove me crazy but didn't
seem to bother others, the interpersonal dynamic a finely tuned
affair. Again, I offered to cook 'for a change' I said, but my offer
was deflected with a giggle and polite refusal, 'Maybe another
time.' Breakfast consisted of macaroni, and for dinner, ravioli.
Most of the day passed as we lay around reading. Some played
chess, others dice games or a board game similar to backgammon.
We didn't play chess often, mainly because of constant fatigue.*

The best chess player in our group, Sergey (cook and magnetologist) challenged Slava, who was skillful, but Sergey was at another
level. I gently enquired whether I might play Sergey, hoping to learn
something and improve my game. My innocent request generated
chuckling all round, and huge grins. Sergey didn't just beat me,
he smashed me out of the park, cornering me in checkmate after
checkmate, usually in a handful of moves. My comrades thought it
hilarious. With each thrashing the comments would flood in, 'See,
we told you he was good, ho, ho ho …' I tried to pick up tips, but
language limitations (and tiredness) prevented meaningful conversation about tactics and strategy.

At 9pm the crashing noise of an opening door preceded, 'Ta
dah'. Then who should shuffle in with a faltering swagger? None
other than Valentine G, swathed in a thick blanket and multiple
layers of gloves, hats and scarf. Slava and Vlad had assisted him

over from the Kharkovchanka. Impressed by Slava's surgical skills, and proud of Valentine's bravery, we welcomed them with a rousing cheer. Valentine sat down tentatively without uttering a word, then joined the board game already underway. He stayed with us for half an hour. If he was in pain, he didn't admit it, although his complexion and demeanour suggested full recovery could be some time away. Slava and Vlad escorted him back to his bunk, concluding a major recovery milestone. We remained at GM25 for longer than usual to minimise discomfort for Valentine during this critical stage of his recovery. I considered the extra time advantageous also, as satellite passes were widely spaced at the time.

> **Sunday 19 February 1984:**
>
> *With Valentine G residing in the Kharkovchanka, I necessarily reduced work activities to bare essentials. During the day, I moved quietly around in the darkened interior, using a flashlight only if necessary. This inevitably led to a couple of blunders, such as my initial attempt to operate the JMR with the antenna disconnected. Valentine's appetite returned quickly. For breakfast he consumed a large serve of porridge and coffee, although he remained unwell, his complexion ash grey.*

I found it difficult to sleep. Constant sniffing all day, all night, snorts, grunts, whines, wheezing, incoherent babbling, groans, cries, coughing, the occasional thunderous end-of-the-world-exploding-snort characteristically associated with an epic self-awakening. Unbelievable! My roommates were heavy smokers. Whether inside or outside, smoking, coughing and spitting continued unabated. After the generator switched off and the lights dimmed, the smoking and conversation continued as if at school camp. Our only discussion topic was how to return safely to Mirny. The discussion went on and on, and on, accompanied by a cacophony of sniffing and hazy, billowing smoke.

Monday 20 February 1984:

I walked over to the Kharkovchanka a little after 8am, eager to investigate the performance of JMR-1. My head ached from passive smoking and lack of sleep.

Despite two months of operations in the field and theoretically homeward bound, my problems with the JMR continued. The latest was a faulty power converter. When I opened the box to investigate, I discovered a broken power lead on the 5 MHz oscillator. Heat-shrink tubing had obscured the break. Although disgusted, I was also elated. Could this be the reason for all of my power problems to date? I removed the DC converter inserted two days earlier. I reclaimed the exchanged oscillator and resoldered a broken connection, then reassembled the components inside the orange box, closed the lid and powered it up. Power supply from the Kharkovchanka remained unreliable. The generator in the balok was unserviceable, switched off for an oil change. I hoped to generate satellite alerts and pre-process a data tape. Voltage tests appeared normal. I scribbled a lengthy telegram to my supervisor describing the latest developments.

Valentine G joined us for dinner, the first time since his operation one week earlier. He had improved noticeably, to the point of moving around comfortably, and he could manage one full hour sitting at the dinner table. Each day he took a short walk outside. Outdoors, the weather was less pleasant. At 11:30pm Sergey (radio operator) entered the balok steaming like a block of dry ice after completing an outdoor task. Sitting down beside us, he declared emphatically, 'The temperature out there … it's -60°C!' Given our official thermometer bottomed out at -53°C and was literally off the scale, we weren't sure exactly how he arrived at this conclusion. We discussed it amongst ourselves, and subsequently agreed -60°C was indeed a reasonable estimate, based on 'feeling'. Travel conditions were poor and did not bode well for our descent to the station. Once past Pionerskaya, ferocious blizzards would hit us again.

Tuesday 21 February 1984:

Kerry's 26th birthday. I tried to make contact via Earl but failed again due to unfavourable propagation conditions. Another major life event missed! Increasingly cold weather also encumbered the vehicles. Yet another serious gearbox malfunction with the ATT delayed departure till 3pm while Serge (mechanic) and Valery investigated and made repairs. Our travel day ceased at 5pm having arrived back at GM13. Valery immediately re-hitched the stores sled that he had left parked-up during the outbound leg. Dinner featured gravy beef stew, beans and tinned tomatoes.

I operated JMR-4 as we travelled during the day to process tapes and determine the quality of the accumulated data. During the day, noise from my printer wasn't noticeable, drowned out by overwhelming engine noise. During the evening however – when the vehicles were stationary – Valentine G found the noise disturbing. I therefore stopped operating the printer in the evening. After dinner we remobilised and travelled overnight to GM12, arriving at 6:30am the following morning.

Wednesday 22 February 1984:

After arriving in the vicinity of GM12, Vlad couldn't find the station mark. The original wooden stake lay buried somewhere unknown, and was re-marked with an un-numbered aluminium pole by the traverse party the previous season. After digging around and examining tags, the correct marker was eventually located. JMR-4 locked on to the first passing satellite and generated an excellent dataset by the end of our stay.

I experimented with Russian clothing again, and commenced wearing the vallinke on a regular basis. At this second attempt I found them remarkably effective and reversed my previous negative opinions. Although now a fan of the vallinke, I still found the process of wrapping my feet with cloth rags to be awkward and unnatural.

A small glitch occurred with track repairs on the ATT when one crawler track completely unravelled and splayed itself flat on the snow surface. Valery manoeuvred the Kharkovchanka in front of the ATT to effect repairs by towing the ATT back onto its track. At 11pm, Sergey (mechanic) and others were still outside, working in rotating shifts, in complete darkness. Valery tried to jumpstart the diesel generator in the balok. It was frozen!

Thursday 23 February 1984:

We hoped to complete track repairs last night, but external temperatures around -60°C precluded meaningful progress. Everyone was dog-tired. Work ceased after I spotted hydraulic oil pouring onto the snow surface, the result of a hydraulic hose bursting while attempting to start the ATT.

Confidence in our vehicles collapsed at that point; the risks were now brutally obvious. Daytime temperatures hovered consistently in the minus 40s with overnight temperatures in the minus 60s. 'These conditions are unusually cold!' remarked Valentine K. Not meaning to state the bleeding obvious, Valentine K was expressing a view that last time he travelled this route he didn't think it was as cold as we were currently experiencing. Similarly, vehicle breakdowns were off the scale in terms of frequency and variety. Sergey (mechanic) worked outside for several hours to coerce frozen oil from a 20-litre drum. His method of lighting a fire fuelled by broken timber crates, then throwing the drum on top was, I thought, innovative, but not very safe. Extreme cold turned Soviet diesel to jelly at those temperatures. Stored in bulk rather than drums, Soviet diesel had a wax point[10] noticeably higher than the aviation turbine kerosene that fuelled Australian Antarctic vehicles. Soviet vehicles coped with poorer quality fuel by using robust preheating systems to warm the whole engine compartment prior to starting.

---

10. Wax point is the temperature at which the paraffin in diesel starts to solidify and bind together.

My JMRs (both of them) also continued to malfunction. Vlad woke me at 11pm to advise the JMR had stopped due to a faulty AC/DC power converter, a fault I could not repair. Sergey's radio also continued to malfunction intermittently. Ten days had elapsed since Valentine G's operation. His condition and energy levels were dramatically improved. Up and about every day with improved demeanour, he even smiled occasionally and was tens of kilograms lighter. We hoped Valentine's condition would continue to improve, but frankly his medical issues were no longer our greatest concern. A greater concern loomed regarding the viability of both prime movers, a life-threatening risk for all.

Faced with a growing list of catastrophes, we appreciated any distraction. During the evening we paused (along with all Soviet Antarctic stations) to celebrate Defender of the Fatherland Day, known today as Red Army and Navy Day. Twenty-three February is a public holiday in Russia and marks the anniversary of the first mass draft of Petrograd and Moscow residents into the Red Army in 1918 during the Russian Civil War. Colloquially, the holiday is also referred to as Men's Day – the counterpart of International Women's Day celebrated on 8 March.

Sergey (cook/magnetologist) prepared a formal meal to the high standards of an ANARE midwinter dinner. Telexes flowed in from other Soviet bases throughout the day. We took turns reading messages aloud, then initiated toasts fuelled by vodka and beer. Amongst them was an emotional tribute to Slava's skill and courage in saving Valentine's life. Slava, a modest person, shied away from comparisons with Leonid Rogosov. But we agreed, unanimously, that Slava also deserved the Order of the Red Banner of Labour.

This same day I also received a telegram from a colleague at Mawson, who forwarded advice on behalf of the Australian Department of Communications. The message informed me that my call sign to date (VK3XTH, or VK0XTH) was no longer valid.

I was instructed to use callsign VK0AG thereafter. The Department claimed I didn't indicate a desire to use high frequency when I applied for a call sign. I certainly thought I had brought this matter to the Department's attention prior to departure without receiving a reply.

Disaster Strikes

Friday 24 February 1984:

We slept until 1pm, still parked at GM12, with all team members feeling the effects of the garrulous celebrations the previous evening. One colleague hopped up twice during the early hours to rush outside and vomit. Very Aussie, I thought!

The JMR recorded less than 12 satisfactory satellite passes due to repeated power failures. Sergey (radio operator) continued the battle with the ever-temperamental 'Old Dedooshka'. It was now incapable of transmitting but could still receive messages. Despite repeated efforts during the day, neither vehicle would start due to the extreme cold. The mechanics battled valiantly until 7pm. One crawler track from the Kharkovchanka remained splayed on the snow all day, and broken track pins lay all around. Our power situation was diabolical: the generators were barely able to produce sufficient current to run my radio. I failed to connect with Earl although I did hear other stations. Every important piece of equipment failed or was in the process of failing: the prime movers, the generators in both the Kharkovchanka and balok, both of my JMR satellite doppler receivers, 'Old Dedooshka' and the Astro C and … the men. Just when we thought it couldn't get worse, it did! TEN TIMES BLOODY WORSE!

Quiet and preoccupied by internal thoughts, Valery was clearly worried. I couldn't tell how much the others knew or passed on. I could only read their body language, and it was bad, very bad. The mechanics had toiled and fiddled with both vehicles for two days now without success. Desperate for parts and desperate for a change of fortune, Valery and Sergey (mechanic) composed a telegram requesting another air drop, this time for compressed air. Outdoor conditions were bone-chilling: winds strengthened, the barometer plummeted, a blizzard was imminent.

My colleagues returned to the balok to rest and thaw out after their long exterior work sessions. Their parkas steamed like dry ice on entry to the warm interior of the living van. Cold air visibly oozed off their parkas and tumbled to the floor. Icy beards, frozen eyebrows and frozen moustaches contained stalactite blobs of ice. Icicles for nose hair adorned each man's face.

Saturday 25 February 1984:

Although not functioning properly, 'Old Dedooshka' still had a surprise in store. Yesterday's SOS message, which we thought had not been received, did in fact get through. Thankfully, an IL14 was on its way. The continuing radio malfunction forced Sergey (radio operator) to rig up a bizarre entanglement of wires whereby the Astro C functioned as the transmitter – for morse code messaging only. Old Dedooshka continued to function as the receiver.

The steady deterioration in weather continued through the morning, resulting by noon in visibility reduced to 100 m. Moderate winds and temperatures decreasing to -45°C confirmed yesterday's omen of an unwelcomed, fully-fledged blizzard. We remained dressed and huddled around the radio throughout the afternoon. All heads were bowed while we waited for news of the aircraft's arrival. Despite having accurate position coordinates for our location, ground drift prevented the aircrew from achieving a confirmed sighting. They circled and searched for hours in our general vicinity but simply couldn't see us. Valery fired flares intermittently to no avail. He resorted again to the old smoke beacon trick, setting fire to oily rags, but the same outcome occurred. Wind and ground drift caused the billowing smoke to ooze along the surface without rising. Valentine G remained huddled under three blankets drawn tightly to his chin, desperately cold despite our best efforts to maintain warmth in the cabin. The constant opening and closing of the doors didn't help.

At times a blurry image of the sun penetrated meekly through the ground drift. We hoped for a break in the weather, sufficient for the air crew to spot us, but the IL14 just continued circling and searching for hours without luck. At 11pm Slava reported glimpses of shadows he believed to be the aircraft. But as the hours ticked away, the odds of them finding us diminished. Eventually the pilot had no choice but to turn back, a depressing outcome for all involved. We had little confidence another flight could or would make a follow-up attempt. The JMR continued to operate, well … sort of. Frustratingly, it wouldn't lock-on to satellites during a blizzard. I couldn't be sure, but I figured 'blizz' static was diminishing the signal strength. The weather forecast for the following day was equally appalling.

At 9pm we received news from Mirny of a revised plan to deliver our desperately needed compressed air and batteries. An aircraft would fly the goods to Komsomolskaya, a mere 500 km away, to be collected by Vostok mechanics who would commandeer two vehicles from the returning Dome B traverse then make a significant detour to deliver them to us, over-snow. The Vostok supply traverse was at the time about 24 hours away from reaching Komsomolskaya. Improvisation had been our saviour to date, but now our survival depended on the actions of others. We had no choice other than to sit tight and wait, most likely for a minimum of five days. Luckily, Kerry knew nothing about our predicament at the time. She was upset at the wharf in Hobart when I boarded *Nella Dan*. What would she think if she understood the extent of this catastrophe? Vlad, Sergey (mechanic) and Valery paced in circles, muttering at each other while debating recovery scenarios. Their unhappy faces portrayed the complete story – all equally downcast and quiet.

Sergey (mechanic) had not given up on improvisation, however. Over dinner he voiced a left-field thought, 'How about we use a fire extinguisher instead of compressed air.' I don't know if he was serious, but he definitely mulled things over. That wry smile emerged again as he fiddled with the fire extinguisher, rotating it in his hands as he mumbled. The next thing we knew, the predictable became reality. The extinguisher triggered accidentally inside the van. Foam spewed everywhere, all over the dining room table and bunk beds, all over my unfortunate colleagues seated next to Serge. The mess triggered a huge kerfuffle of swearing and finger pointing.

A curtailed science program was inevitable now. Once the Dome B traverse arrived, we'd make a run for home, non-stop. I had no misgivings or regrets. JMR-4 continued to malfunction constantly. The 400 MHz channel dropped out, test voltages were nonsense and the printer refused to work.

Sunday 26 February 1984:

Despite resoldering several weak joints. I did not solve the recurring problems with JMR-4. The instrument appeared to function correctly until I connected the printer. Then it became unserviceable. Out of sheer desperation I powered up JMR-1 hoping for a miracle, and guess what, it worked normally as if nothing had happened! This was a miracle!

The weather also improved. Yesterday's wind and drift disappeared. Temperatures were in the low minus 40s. Valery was back working on the Kharkovchanka, still experimenting with methods to make it start. The balok generator received attention following input from Valentine G, who seemed much improved and back to normal.

At this point Vlad voiced a suggestion, 'We have 24 hours to fix the vehicles. Let's charge four batteries from both vehicles using the balok's diesel generator for about 20 hours, then try to start the

Kharkovchanka using all four batteries. If successful, we can pump compressed air into the ATT tanks and also start the ATT.'

I finished reading *Dune 2* and commenced *Lenin and the Bolsheviks*, to the delight of my tovarischee (comrades), but I could not maintain concentration. My fingers turned the pages. My eyes passed over the words, but every now and then I would stop and realise that I'd failed to absorb anything.

Around midnight Slava and Sergey (mechanic) burst through the balok door again, shrieking, 'Let's go, let's go!' I had no idea what this meant until I stepped outside. The Kharkovchanka's head lights beamed, the engine was revving hard. Sergey (mechanic) and Valery had worked stubbornly all night to eventually start the ATT. I don't know how they did it, but none of us cared. Sergey (radio operator) also had a win. He somehow managed to conjure repairs to Old Dedooshka to render it serviceable again. Vlad advised Mirny immediately and cancelled the rescue mission from Komsomolskaya. Suddenly we had a glimmer of hope. We devoured breakfast and hurried to move out. Serge (mechanic) hadn't slept for days and looked like a dead man walking.

Monday 27 February 1984:

Although mobile, the crippled ATT streamed dark liquid in its tracks. Lubricant stocks dwindled to almost zero. Only two drums of engine oil remained, plus one drum of antifreeze.

Throughout our traverse, the ATT and Kharkovchanka often travelled separately without concern, frequently losing visual contact. Now, with the ATT in disrepair, both vehicles remained, or tried to remain, within sight of each other – a difficult feat in heavy drift and limited visibility – at times down to one hundred metres or less. Amazingly, we carried no form of voice communication (such as VHF radios) between vehicles, and no radar. Serge (mechanic) carried the one and only flare gun, with instructions from Valery to signal by firing a flare should the ATT breakdown or stop. Leaking oil caused periodic flames to flare from the ATT engine, so Vlad decided to ride in the cabin and watch the open engine compartment, fire extinguisher in hand, ready to use if needed. We paused for lunch at 1:30pm. Utterly spent, Valery collapsed and fell asleep immediately. Sergey (radio operator) updated Mirny. I checked the JMR. The clock had stopped and the receiver power light was out. I gave up being gentle and thumped it with my fist. Bingo, everything worked normally again. *Forget the soldering iron*, I thought, *just thump it!*

Despite obvious exhaustion, Sergey (mechanic) soldiered on, attending to ATT maintenance. Although some distance away, I noticed his difficulty handling a 20-litre oil drum. I wandered over to offer assistance, some might say stickybeak. Extreme cold had transformed the normally free-flowing engine oil into a thick non-flowing gooey ooze. To speed up extraction, Serge had decided to heat the exterior of the drum by applying direct flame from an LP gas burner. *Interesting*, I thought. He was seated with the drum over one knee, his other arm wrapped around the outside, the opening pointed down. With his free arm, Serge ignited the gas while simultaneously holding the burner, then proceeded to stroke the flame gently up and down the exterior, rotating the drum as he progressed.

I wondered whether he'd done this before. 'Is this common practice?' I asked. Every now and then, he'd look up and grin mischievously. 'Obviously not!' The flame, although the strength of a candle, generated a surprising amount of heat – sufficient to encourage the gelatinous contents to flow more quickly. The oil emerged like a thick jelly snake, but not fast enough for Sergey, who became impatient. To hasten matters, he intermittently moved the flame from the outside of the drum directly onto the emerging ooze itself, grinning all the while. At this point I decided to leave! When next I saw Sergey – approximately one hour later over dinner – his face was black, eyebrows nearly completely removed. His hair was significantly singed! 'The oil drum had exploded when flame ignited a gas bubble trapped inside,' confided Serge. 'Bang …' He was lucky to survive. I didn't ask what happened to our precious last quantities of oil! Over dinner, the conversation returned again to the strategy for our safe return to Mirny. If we could reach it, Pionerskaya was the goal, an important staging point with abundant supplies of oil and lubricants. With any luck, the Dome B team might be waiting for us.

Valentine G relocated to the balok; a wise decision given the superior ride. I elected to also remain in the balok. Everyone slept soundly, exhausted by the stress of recent breakdowns and invasive cold. The latest update on aircraft movements from Mirny advised, 'The IL14 is unable to leave Mirny due to bad weather,' so we just kept crawling along, slowly and steadily. I fell asleep, but during the early hours of the morning woke to an eerie silence. The vehicles had stopped moving.

Emergency, Emergency, Emergency

Tuesday 28 February 1984:

At midday I discovered the reason for halting. I hadn't paid attention to the conversation at breakfast. I couldn't understand why everyone looked despondent. Overnight, the ATT had dropped way behind and then broken down again … something to do with the clutch or flywheel. But this time, it was really serious! Valery (in the Kharkovchanka) paused for hours to let the ATT catch up. By the time I woke, Sergey (mechanic) and Valery were fast asleep. Although late getting started, Serge hauled himself out of bed to continue repairs on the ATT. Valery meanwhile, turned his attention to the balok generator. Vlad was scribbling feverishly, preparing another urgent telegram. Sergey (cook) retrieved a large collection of canned meat from a storage compartment underneath the bunk beds in the balok. 'Hmmm … are we about to start walking?' I wondered.

Lack of spare parts and tools was another emerging problem. I was shocked when Valery asked if he could 'borrow' my toolkit. 'Borrow my toolkit? I exclaimed. 'Don't you realise, all I have are things like a soldering iron, pliers, spanners, screwdrivers and so on'. 'Da, spaceeba,' he said as he rushed out with it. I later walked over to the balok to find a mini production line in full swing. Our dinner table (the same one used for the appendicectomy) was now a functioning workbench to manufacture brushes for the balok generator. Amid a disassembled range of generator parts, several guys were fashioning lead and copper wire around the stator coil. This was the start of an unbelievable sequence of breakdowns that made the events to date seem like child's play.

The next disaster occurred when Valery tried to 'break out' from our overnight parking position. Exuberant jerking by the Kharkovchanka on the sleds caused one of the crawler tracks to break again. Repositioning the balok behind the fuel sled had created significantly heavier tow loads. The Kharkovchanka stopped moving when one track disintegrated, but the balok did not. It kept sliding, right up onto and over the splayed growsers of the Kharkovchanka's missing track. Subsequent repairs took hours and required the extraction and replacement of dozens of broken track pins.

In the next attempt to break out, a pivotal 'D-shackle' – a connection between the tow bar and the cable – snapped unexpectedly. Ordinarily, this would not cause anxiety, but everything seemed to be breaking. Valery (mechanic) became despondent. He assumed the worst. Initially, he thought the eye of the drawbar had snapped. He wasn't sure because the towing tackle was buried in snow. Luckily, only the D-shackle broke, an item easily replaced. Later that evening, several of us were sitting in the Kharkovchanka when the door flew open again and all hell broke loose. Man ... this was unbelievable. What now? Sergey (mechanic) was screaming, absolutely SCREAMING! 'Poshar, poshar' ... Fire, fire! *Bloody hell ... Fire!*

What happened next was astonishing. Bear in mind, the outside temperature was in the minus 50s. Valery leaped up without donning cold weather clothing. He grabbed a fire extinguisher from the wall and ran out the door dressed in the equivalent of casual office attire. Others followed in various stages of half-dress, Vlad amongst them. I decided at least one person should be properly dressed, in case the others froze and had to be dragged inside. The fire was extinguished by the time I'd thrown on clothing and jogged over. The guys were standing around the ATT, nonchalant and relatively relaxed, nattering and scratching their heads, and it was still in the minus 50s. The emergency was under control, but the consequences were far from over. After dinner, we debated (i.e. the others debated while I listened and tried to follow) the extent of details to share with our rescuers in the returning Vostok party. From what I could understand, Vlad had received strong advice from Lebedev – the leader of the Vostok traverse – to abandon the ATT and head directly for Pionerskaya. However, our team's decision was, 'Let's sleep on it and make one final attempt to start the ATT in the morning.'

Lebedev – an experienced polyarnik, had 'lost count of the number of times he'd been to Antarctica', according to Vlad. Amongst other polar accomplishments, he was a mechanic/driver on the legendary Soviet expedition of 1966 that travelled from Vostok to Molodezhnaya via the Pole of Relative Inaccessibility, a staggering 5,000 km accomplished with three tractor trains. Apparently, they ran out of fuel 500 km from Molodezhnaya and waited for one week for fuel to be flown out, delayed in the meantime by a combination of poor weather and yet another case of appendicitis at the station.

Wednesday 29 February 1984:

Daylight inspection of the ATT revealed an irrepairable cracked oil tank. The oil leak extended into the preheating ducts, explaining the over-snow oil trail, and the cause of the fire. Effective immediately, the ATT was dead to us. Our position at the time was 3 km west of GM11 (72° 35'S, 107° 20'E). During the 2pm radio sked' with Mirny, we discussed and agreed to abandon the ATT and dash for Pionerskaya in one tractor train. Hopefully, the Vostok team would be waiting for us. Sergey (mechanic) was heartbroken. His pride was deeply wounded by this turn of events. He refused to eat lunch and languished around the ATT as if his pet dog had died. His eyeballs were bloodshot red, with big dark bags under his eye sockets from lack of sleep.

Fortunately, the weather improved. The bone-chilling wind subsided, and temperatures hovered around a relatively warm -40°C. The first task involved rearranging cargo. We drained fuel from all the drums remaining on the ATT tray. We removed all the batteries, along with a radio and the block and tackle rig attached to the front bumper. We packed items detached from the ATT on the fuel sled or inside the Kharkovchanka. Sergey (mechanic) prepared 'last rites' for the ATT with the empathy and devotion of an undertaker; it was cruel to watch. He tied back the engine bonnet to prevent the compartment filling with snow, then he opened and tied back the cabin doors to minimise drift snow filling the cabin.

Most of us rode in the balok, hitched immediately behind the Kharkovchanka, with the fuel sled following at the rear. The new towing arrangement provided amazing stability for passengers in the balok. We no longer suffered the crashing and bashing, nor the unpleasant swaying to and fro experienced previously. The dead weight of the fuel sled acted in the way a sea anchor assists yachts in heavy seas. It stabilised the movement of the balok. The new ride was unbelievably smooth.

Thursday 1 March 1984:

We drove all day and night, rotating drivers and stopping only for meals. Lunch at 4pm, dinner at midnight. Meal labels were meaningless ... it was a food stop. Our midnight stop coincided with a quick check of an ARMS. Valentine K and Vlad were relieved to find everything in order, thus avoiding a dilemma about whether to halt overnight.

Mundane travel days followed. Our activities as passengers were limited to reading books and listening to music. I tried to contact Earl during a meal break, but radio conditions were terrible. Valentine G's operation, only two weeks previous, felt like an eternity ago. It was now almost forgotten, replaced by weightier concerns about the disintegration of our prime movers and sleds. Valentine's strong improvement actually worried us, due to his tendency for exuberance and over-confidence. Slava instructed Valentine to remain indoors, which Valentine used wisely to study and catalogue my music cassettes, apparently intent on redeploying them on return to Mirny.

The heavier tow load reduced Kharkovchanka to first gear, constraining speed to 7 km/h. We also had another injury to manage. Sergey (cook/magnetologist) reported a deteriorating back condition. Apparently, the injury had beleaguered him since departure, but he had remained silent, until now. He could barely hobble first thing in the morning but continued active kitchen duties. With one arm akimbo for support, and regular applications of 'tiger balm' in the evening to ease discomfort, he had no choice other than to tolerate it.

Friday 2 March 1984:

The breakfast stop of two hours at pole marker 210 placed us 420 km from Pionerskaya. Fine, sunny weather swathed the firm icy snow surface. Overnight temperatures plunged to -47°C. Shallow sledge tracks 100 mm deep contrasted starkly with the 400 mm to 500 mm ruts generated closer to Dome C. At breakfast, I rustled through our groceries gathered at Dome C and found a can of freeze-dried cottage cheese. I reconstituted this immediately and mixed it with tuna and a sprinkling of 'axe-ground' pepper. Although hoping to impress my colleagues with a taste sensation ... I shouldn't have been surprised when they refused to try it. My pleas were rebuffed with raised eyebrows and polite asides such as 'originalna!'

At 2pm, worrying news arrived via a poor-quality radio sked'. Vlad believed he had heard someone announce the breakdown of Lebedev's party, who were now stranded 200 km from Pionerskaya. We were at pole 195, 390 km from Pionerskaya which put the would-be rescue party 190 km away – approximately two days' travel. At this point it looked as though we might become the new rescuing party, not the party requiring rescue.

At 6pm, I tried to contact Earl. I put down the mike to catch up with Vlad regarding news from Lebedev and the Vostok team. That was the moment I heard a dull roar erupt outside, different from anything in recent weeks, and most definitely not the familiar sound of an IL14.

One of the tractor trains in the widely spread Vostok party had heard the earlier radio conversation between Vlad and Lebedev and realised they were extremely close to our location. With no time to waste and without being able to inform us, three expeditioners jumped into the cabin of an ATT and zoomed over to intercept us. Language limitations prevented me from understanding exact details of the rescue operation. A momentary period of stunned silence transformed at warp speed as we rushed outside to investigate the noise. Unbelievable, another miracle! Jubilant introductions and handshakes followed by vigorous hugs accompanied overwhelming joy and relief. Despite my limited language skills, even I babbled in incoherent Russian from the emotion of the moment. With greetings and introductions out of the way, we retreated indoors. Anecdotes and stories gushed out, everyone flabbergasted by our misfortune. 'Totally awesome' is the only phrase to describe the way these guys handled adversity in such an unforgiving environment.

But now, our dilemma was figuring out who was rescuing whom. We still hoped and planned to rendezvous with the Dome B team.

This turn of events became a pleasant conundrum as we devoured coffee and a bellyful of carbohydrates and protein. The incoming ATT-21 took over towing our fuel sled. The Kharkovchanka towed the balok only. Lighter sled loads allowed the Kharkovchanka to engage second gear and increase its average speed to 10 km/h. Off we went like nothing had happened, travelling through the night to reach GM10 by the early hours of the following morning. Arrival of new personalities had an immediate and positive impact on morale and interpersonal dynamics. New people meant a redistribution of duties and new routines as we merged into a new team. I dozed off lying on my bunk, fully clothed in cold weather garb with boots laced, too drained to be bothered changing.

Saturday 3 March 1984:

Our workday commenced at 8am. We collected pieces of a disassembled magnetic station, hammered track pins and redistributed sled loads. The temperature, a chilly -51°C, forced us inside to warm our hands on a regular basis until departure at 9:15am. The balance of the Vostok team were definitely waiting for us at Pionerskaya, 320 km away.

Lebedev – who oversaw all Vostok traverse field operations, now assumed command over our movements. By dinner we'd covered 60 km in six hours, travelling from 9:15am to 3:10pm. The rock-hard surface prevented sled runners and track growsers from scratching the surface. The banging, rolling and crashing of the sleds – akin to a yacht voyage in gale-force winds – made it difficult to rest while underway. By evening, familiar events halted progress again when Kharkovchanka-1, driven by Lebedev's party, threw a track. I also experienced my first close encounter with frostbite while taking photographs of crawler track repairs. I stupidly allowed my fingers to remain ungloved for too long and failed to notice my fingertips turning white. I moved inside to warm up, where my fingers stung like severe sunburn, the pads especially tender.

We also learned that one of the IL14's at Komsomolskaya had broken a piston. Repairs could not proceed until next season. Mirny air operations were reduced to one serviceable IL14.

Sunday 4 March 1984:

We continued all day, stopping at GM07, still 120 km from Pionerskaya. As we pulled up, Valentine G began to dress hurriedly. I wasn't the only person to wonder why. Valentine grabbed a shovel as he raced out the door before anyone commented or challenged him. He stomped off characteristically in the direction of the magnetic station. 'He must think he is recovered?' I thought. Less than half an hour later he scurried back, calling for the doctor and complaining about his stomach wound opening! We stopped many times during the night, and from the warm comfort of my bunk, I could hear the cold noise of track pins being hammered. By 7:30am we'd arrived at a location 4 km from Pionerskaya, where a mass encampment of Vostok traverse vehicles lay waiting. Half an hour later Kharkovchanka-3 from the Dome B traverse arrived in a rolling cloud of swirling drift snow.

Monday 5 March 1984:

A leisurely day followed. Life felt good. We waited for lunch at 3pm which mutated into a huge party in one of the Kharkovchankas. Twenty-three personnel from three traverse teams crammed into a living area designed to comfortably seat eight. Perfect! Some of the boys were drinking and bleary eyed before lunch.

Valentine G entertained comrades by performing handstands. Who could blame him? He was alive against the odds! In contrast to our last party, this celebration involved lavish foods. We savoured exotic flavours including lamb, steak, cabbage soup and bread rolls. At 8pm, events escalated inside the balok. Dim lighting augmented by clouds of cigarette smoke resulted in the bluesy ambience of a Moscow basement jazz club. A guitar made its way around, strummed by anyone interested. Most of the men were novices, some were okay, most weren't, all were enthusiastic and, dare I say, tipsy enough to have a go. Each corner of the balok resembled a mini–Speakers Corner – separate conversations with separate toasts to all manner of identities and icons, peppered with intermittent utterances such as 'Vee wippet' (a small drink), 'Echoo echoo' (a little bit more), all culminating with 'Na zdorovya ...' (your health).

Tuesday 6 March 1984:

The day continued in the same vein as yesterday, utterly no movement until 3pm. We travelled through a short night of pitch-black conditions. Although the thermometer registered warmer days and nights (around -35°C), lower altitudes brought a likelihood of more frequent blizzards. Thus, we continued to feel as cold as ever with the increased windchill more than compensating for theoretically warmer air temperatures.

Another short stop for midnight dinner ... pasta again. Our driver left the balok prematurely after eating and returned to the prime mover while the remainder of us continued eating. Suddenly, the balok jolted forward – a normal break-out practice after a long stop, but one that usually occurred when all individuals were aware and properly prepared. On this occasion, the dinner table remained loaded. The series of hefty jolts occurred without warning and caused water, food and dishes to spill onto the floor, triggering yet another spate of furious swearing.

Wednesday 7 March 1984:

A breakfast stop at 8:30am at GM04 brought welcome relief to the bronco ride overnight that had tossed items all over the van interior.

Rough terrain continued all day. The prime mover gnashed gears in an epic struggle to maintain momentum through the challenging terrain. Every now and then one of us would get up and stagger to shut a door or close a cupboard drawer, or pick up items hurled onto the floor, or to check, for example, that the portable heater had not been smashed. Our new convoy included several broken down 'Vostok' prime movers under tow, amongst them Lebedev's Kharkovchanka 1 and Kharkovchanka 4.

Thursday 8 March 1984:

Our train was mobile at 8am, one of the last to move out. Destination Mirny crept closer, now within 200 km or 3 days travel. Daily temperatures hovered around -24°C, which honestly felt like the tropics after spending weeks in the minus 40s and 50s. Prevalent wind and ever-swirling drift snow exerted a different form of unpleasantness. The swirling drift invaded every nook and cranny of our parkas, icing beards, eyebrows and eyelashes. Increased glare limited our vision. Vehicles and sleds covered themselves in dirty, slushy patches of muddied ice and refrozen snow. Most of us no longer cared or thought about work – we were busy daydreaming about activities at the station. I dreamt of a banya, clean clothes, light footwear (I never want to wear boots again) and ocean views, anything with a bit of colour.

Our late start became an issue when whiteout caused our driver to lose sight of preceding tractor train tracks. He could only see several metres ahead. On numerous occasions the tracks we followed became invisible due to drift snow filling the track ruts. This last section into the station was particularly dangerous. We tried to follow the Vostok team, but whiteout prevented us from maintaining proximity. On several occasions we crossed remnants of old tracks that seemed to head in contradictory directions. The sastrugi direction (or lack of it) played tricks with our navigation. We stopped frequently to examine the surface on foot.

Friday 9 March 1984:

Finally, the whiteout cleared to reveal clear skies and titanium shades of freshly fallen coastal snow. The clearing weather allowed us to enjoy the final run of 105 km into the station proper. Sixty-five kilometres from Mirny we caught glimpses of the coast. Dispersed icebergs dotted the horizon amid ultramarine shades of deep ocean. I collected several snow samples but otherwise had no further work tasks. Our final overnight stop 25 km out from Mirny was planned to ensure we arrived at the station proper during the late morning. We played a game called Nadi and tried to sleep.

Saturday 10 March 1984:

Because of the unusual events we endured, our return to Mirny was eagerly anticipated by station members. A solitary IL14 swooped by to greet us on its way to Molodezhnaya.

The last few kilometres were hilly and difficult, threading our way carefully through the crevasse field. The revving engine and clashing gears of the Kharkovchanka testament to our struggle to maintain traction while dodging occasional rocks and slipping sideways across ice. When the welcoming group from Mirny arrived to greet us, we revelled in the opportunity to stretch our legs. I recognised several personalities from Vostok. We celebrated with vodka, bread and cheese and numerous photos.

As we cruised into the station, our pride collapsed ingloriously as a result of an incident at the base of Dom Radio. While parking the sleds, the trailing balok jack-knifed ahead of the Kharkovchanka. Antennas on both the vehicle and balok tangled with and badly stretched the station's overhead power lines. The power lines (as if acting in retribution) ripped antennas from the roof of our vehicles. Worst of all, the immediate clean-up delayed our arrival at lunch.

During the afternoon I enjoyed a banya, which included an authentic whipping with birch branches, followed by a roll in the snow au naturel, while absorbing stunning views of icebergs from the powerhouse landing adjacent to the banya. I remeasured my weight – 70kg, 0.4kg heavier than my weight prior to departure.

Mirny felt like a bustling, overcrowded township, bursting with activity and energised by outgoing expeditioners. We reconvened in the slightly wounded balok to celebrate our safe return and toast the success of the science program. Several visitors dropped by, amongst them Mirny's chief cook. Unfortunately, I overindulged. I fell asleep in the balok, where I stayed until I sobered up. I left in the early hours before others woke, and returned to my room in Dom Geophisiki.

CHAPTER 6

The Waiting Room

YAHIB YODAK Baikal YIKAL

All are safe and well. Waiting arrival of Baikal. Rather fed up at having to stick around the station/field camp.

Sunday 11 March 1984 to Sunday 18 March 1984:

Demobilising personal possessions and equipment from the Kharkovchanka occupied an entire day. I moved everything to my allocated room (No. 3 at Dom Geophisiki, the Science Block). I emptied drawers and shelves and packed up antennas, tools, books, personal clothing, batteries and cold weather garments. I derigged the Astro C and disassembled both JMRs. I packed instruments and belongings into their respective travel cases.

Dom Geophisiki was 500 metres downslope from Dom Radio (the mess/main accommodation building). The vehicle workshop and powerhouse buildings were located further downslope.

During the evening Mikhail (radio operator from Vostok) visited me from his assigned residence in a retired Kharkovchanka parked halfway between Dom Radio and Dom Geophisiki. The now decommissioned Kharkovchanka served two purposes for Mikhail: both accommodation and radio shack. We chatted in a mixture of English and Russian and scanned the amateur bands listening to snippets of various conversations. I sent a CQ call to 'Melbourne' but didn't receive an immediate response. Later I heard a faint, crackling noise of a VK3 station trying to break through. Despite the late hour and poor propagation conditions, Earl made contact and immediately insisted on calling Kerry. But Kerry was unavailable again, and I missed another opportunity to speak to her. I returned to my room rather late and caused alarm bells when a vigilant neighbour noticed I wasn't back at 11pm. Acting responsibly, he rang the OIC to enquire about my whereabouts and expressed concern for my safety.

The incoming officer in charge – a magnetologist by profession named Dmitriev – had commenced his ninth wintering expedition at Mirny, the fifth as officer-in-charge. Dmitriev took over station command from Serdyukov during our period away. On Monday I tracked down Dmitriev to introduce myself, thinking I'd be sailing home within days. I wanted to check on the progress of a request I'd left with Serdyukov, before departing for Dome C, for temperature records to send back to the head of our Glaciology Section in Melbourne. After dinner, I sat through a Russian science fiction film screened in the mess. Although unable to follow the dialogue, I enjoyed the theatre of it. The cinematic effects included angry eyes; staring, fearful and hateful faces; trembling hands – sudden close-ups of trembling hands to heighten suspenseful moments; and big stares! The effects were hypnotic. The acting dramatic, suspenseful, and neither better nor worse … but different from Hollywood productions. But then, it was science fiction! I found the experience of ignoring dialogue strangely liberating, and different from watching a silent movie. I certainly didn't feel I'd missed anything by not following the dialogue. I could plainly see where the story was going and enjoyed watching the audience engagement and reactions. After the film finished, I called in to see Mikhail (radio operator) on my walk back to Dom Geophisiki.

At night, the illuminated path between Dom Radio and Dom Geophisiki featured alternately coloured lights, two white and one red light attached sequentially to a catenary wire supported by stakes positioned along the entire 500 m path. Fierce winds often scoured loose snow from the track, leaving it glassy and slippery like a skating rink. Swirling drift snow obscured visibility on regular occasions, causing difficulties staying upright in strong winds. Even if holding on to the 'blizz line'*, one could be upended at any moment, risking a twisted ankle, twisted knee or broken bone. When tramping it three times a day you soon realised it was a considerable amount of daily exercise. The worst aspect was the fuss involved in kitting up. First the parka, then padded trousers, balaclava, gloves and boots, then removing it all at the other end, re-donning it for the return walk, then removing it all again. Dressing up and dressing down was tedious and time-consuming. You couldn't afford to go outside without wind-proofs because the weather could change quickly and you didn't want to be caught out. And yet, occasionally someone would run the gauntlet without dressing appropriately.

My room in Dom Geophisiki was comfortable and quarantined from the whiffy odour that characterised rooms in Dom Radio.

On Tuesday I assisted Mikhail to rig up a delta-loop antenna, then walked to our balok for a 5pm appointment to celebrate 'one-month since Valentine's operation'. I left the party one hour later for the sked' with Earl and, to my surprise, Kerry was available. We talked for an hour, after which I had dinner in the Meteorology shack at Anton's invitation to celebrate his 23rd birthday. It was a great night of singing, accompanied by guitars and a piano accor-dion. Kerry reminds me frequently that all she remembers me talking about was the need to go and have dinner.

The following day Vlad called in to ensure I'd heard a station announcement, 'The banya is working!' My room being adjacent to both the powerhouse and banya meant that, if I moved quickly, I could get in without waiting. I quickly gathered a pile of soiled clothes and spent the remainder of the morning washing myself and my clothes. Ablutions, clothes washing and room cleaning were personal and fully manual chores. To the best of my knowledge, the station did not have a washing machine, nor clothes pegs, dryers or lines – in the banya, or elsewhere. I took wet washing to my room to dry by draping garments over criss-crossing string lines. I placed some items, such as thick socks, directly on the column heater.

After several days of 'kicking back', I felt I needed to confirm the quality of JMR data collected during the traverse. I couldn't do anything about it if the data was corrupt, but I was keen to confirm that I'd achieved the plan. I rigged up JMR-4 to function as a microprocessor and counted the number of satisfactory satellite passes at each station. All good.

Over the weekend colleagues provided me with updated news of the expected arrival date for the *Baikal*. It was due into Mirny on 4 April 1984 – only a couple of weeks away. Saturday's whiteout deteriorated by Sunday into raging blizzard. Normally from the window in my room I could see Dom Radio at the top of the hill. As of 9am Sunday, Dom Radio was totally invisible.

Attending meals in the mess meant clinging to the blizz line, clawing your way while leaning into the wind, occasionally turning your head for a glimpse of your location and falling, often skating and stumbling onto all fours, then sliding and crawling, and finally swearing about a banged knee or other indignities. After several trips through appalling weather, I noticed an absence of familiar faces. At first, I thought my colleagues must be attending a separate mess as Dom Geophisiki residents were scientists and technicians. Did they have a kitchen I didn't know about? I soon learned of the long-standing tradition for many guys to fry potatoes and onions in their room on a portable electric hotplate rather than endure the slippery slope to the mess for a particularly ordinary reward. Self-catering didn't happen at every meal, but was common. Every now and then individuals would tramp to the warehouse and return with bags with potatoes and onions. After hearing about this practice, being naturally inquisitive, I decided to visit the store and investigate for myself.

On arrival at the store, I first noticed an abacus on the counter, a portent. Beyond the counter my eyes ballooned at the sight of a mini-mountain of black/dark green potatoes, mostly shrivelled, ugly, wrinkly specimens covered with sprouting, long hairy shoots. The idea of self-catering suddenly lost its appeal, even though the kitchen obviously drew down from the same provisions. Mess meals commonly featured a bland combination of mashed potato, rice, buckwheat or spaghetti with a lump of meat, usually stewed. Occasionally, meatballs were served with bread. The bread wasn't too bad. Salt was the only condiment available: no pepper. Beverage options consisted of tea or water. Dessert was unusual and rarely offered. No cakes other than an occasional pastry, no green vegetables, no fresh fruit. Breakfast was typically a bowl of porridge, or bread (hard, chewy white bread) and a cup of tea. The only difference between lunch and dinner was butter – available with dinner, but almost never at lunchtime.

Monday 19 March 1984 to Sunday 25 March 1984:

Blizzard raged through the entire weekend then weakened by Monday into strong winds with associated mist. The latest update on the Baikal's arrival indicated further delay, slipping out to 8 April.

The wind softened on Tuesday and blue skies emerged. My morning also improved with an unexpected visit from a small group including Slava. We walked to a caravan on the other side of Dom Radio to join two outgoing Vostok expeditioners and to celebrate our hopefully imminent departure with tea and shortbreads. During the afternoon I watched a matinee screened in the mess. I still couldn't follow the dialogue but once again enjoyed the 'theatre' experience.

I also began reading (in English) several Russian novels I had brought from Australia. I felt no compunction about lying around reading. After all, I'd just spent every hour of every day, seven days a week for the previous three months, 'at work' – one year's full-time equivalent work hours achieved in the space of three months. My reading campaign began with Dostoyevsky's *The Brothers Karamazov*, a weird but thoroughly enjoyable masterpiece. I followed this with Tolstoy's *War and Peace*, reading it from cover to cover with only one false start. Once I had grasped the characters' names, I found the story engrossing and could hardly put it down. Next, I tackled Dostoevsky's *Crime and Punishment* – my eyes were glued to every page. It was the best novel I'd read at the time. I continued reading for most days until departure, apart from interruptions to perform an occasional work task, such as hand copying snow accumulation data for Vlad to pass to the Russian glaciology group in Moscow.

On Friday evening I played chess and a card game called 'Preference', similar to 500. A dreadful week of high winds and blizzard deteriorated over the weekend into whiteout propelled by mindboggling, howling winds. Dom Geophisiki shook violently. My room (located on the windward side) leached all warmth as the paltry column heater struggled to cope. I wondered how anyone could survive winter here. It was so, so, so cold.

Monday 26 March 1984 to Sunday 1 April 1984:

Thankfully, Monday was warm and sunny. I set off joyfully to take photos around the station with nothing off-limits. I mostly captured indoor scenes of laboratories, the kitchen, sleeping quarters, the mess, library and offices.

Whereas conversation at Australian Antarctic stations continuously analysed, discussed and evaluated the quality of meals, I do not recall meals ever being a topic of conversation at Mirny. Rather, food was a matter of grim acceptance and never discussed. However, one evening meal deserves special mention. While waiting at the hole-in-the-wall servery, my eyes popped at what I perceived, or imagined, to be a mega-sized serving of beefsteak covered with thick lashings of chunky gravy. Wanting to believe my eyes, I salivated immediately like Pavlov's dog but I should have known better. Slicing into what I thought was beefsteak I discovered it to be … liver. Thick, tough, fried liver plonked on top of boiled (not mashed) potato with a side serving of preserved cabbage. Even the delicious-looking gravy reeked of liver aftertaste and was not the least bit appetising. I gagged at the first mouthful then promptly moved my plate to one side and filled up on bread and butter washed down with weak black tea.

I also made another effort to consume 'kvas' – the traditional Russian beverage made from fermented rye bread, or alternatively brewed from wheat, rye or barley. Try as I might, I never liked kvas – I found it to be an acquired taste. I preferred beer. Altogether I did not eat well at Mirny. Most meals involved monotonous pork, liver or kidney, with side servings of boiled potato, cold beans and pickled cabbage accompanied by bread, bread and more bread. After dinner I watched another movie in the mess. This time it was a black-and-white detective movie produced in 1982 with a story involving bandits in a truck (not car) chase. They kill a female payroll clerk and are chased Keystone cop–like through the countryside in various groups of twos and threes.

Arrival information for *Baikal* suggested continuing delays. The vessel was at least one more week away. Strong winds at Molodezhnaya had also delayed the unloading of the *Kapitan Gotsky*. Vlad and I were privileged to be invited to visit Lebedev, who gave me several stamped envelopes to take home for collectors. My other achievement for the day involved taking a banya.

Monday 2 April 1984 to Sunday 8 April 1984:

Life at Mirny slowed as we waited further confirmation of Baikal's arrival date. Now well into autumn, and unusually late to be welcoming a resupply ship (i.e. any resupply ship, much less one that is not an ice breaker), our departure prospects did not look good. Station gossip exploded amongst nervous groups gathered around maps. Various stories emerged about the current whereabouts of both ships and the increased likelihood of spending the approaching winter stranded at Mirny.

The weather doubled down and continued to deteriorate. Blizz days became more frequent and the quality of station life deteriorated accordingly. The sea ice at Mirny started to build and thicken noticeably, making it tricky for vessels lacking an ice-strengthened hull. Pinned down day after day by howling, monotonous blizzards, all outgoing expeditioners were on a knife edge, pondering and muttering about our predicament. The excessive idle time resulted in oddball queries and conversations directed to me about life in Australia: 'How do you pawn a camera?', 'What is the price of beer, wine, cigarettes and jeans?' Another asked 'How many varieties of mushrooms exist in Australia?', which made me wonder … what had he been eating? I was interrogated for suggestions on souvenirs costing less than 10 dollars.

Almost every day someone approached me with a swap request (which loosely translated meant 'give away') for my padded overalls and accessories including my personal watch, camera and boots. On one occasion, a gruff character who normally avoided eye contact, and to whom I hadn't spoken previously, approached me in the mess. I was eating at the time. He had obviously been drinking. He leaned over and whispered in my ear to avoid being overheard. He requested a can of beer, to which I responded truthfully, 'Sorry, I don't have any beer.' Swaying for a second or two while glowering at me eyeball to eyeball, he swivelled round in disbelief. Then … without uttering a word, he marched off in umbrage. During my final weeks, I received dozens of swap requests from individuals I hadn't met and didn't know. I felt uncomfortable about this and decided to politely decline everyone. I saved one item until the last moment – a bottle of Southern Comfort presented to me at Mawson. During this last week I felt the timing was right to share a toast with my neighbours in Dom Geophisiki – a small but well-received gesture that stretched to four rounds of small shots for 10 or 11 people.

Thursday 5 April was also a day to remember. I spoke to Kerry (in Melbourne) by amateur radio relayed in messages through an operator named 'Doc', located in Byron Bay.

The following day we received another update about the *Baikal*, informing us that *Baikal*'s passengers had been offloaded to another vessel, the *Professor Vise*. The *Baikal* was definitely on its way to Mirny with an expected arrival date now of 10 April. It seemed I would be dropped off in Fremantle about 20 April, incredibly late in the season.

Strong winds on Saturday (25 to 30 m/s, or 50 to 60 knots) made the 'promenade' between Dom Geophisiki and Dom Radio extremely icy and dangerous. Time passed slowly. I continued to read and read. Occasionally I met colleagues for a cup of tea and polite conversation, which usually doubled as a tutorial in conversational English. The pressure to swap everyday objects continued and now included my rucksack and winter boots. The next couple of days were a little bit blurry.

After a dinner featuring (drumroll please) fish and mashed potato, Vlad and I attended drinks with the OIC. I took a bottle of Australian red – the last of my alcohol supplies - which supplemented the usual Ararat brandy and champagne. We were also treated to tasty snacks of a quality much higher than the fare available in the mess. Guests included Alex, the ice-coring operator to whom I was introduced at Vostok; Boris, the second in charge at Vostok; and Sasha, chief of the Dome B traverse. I chatted to Sasha for some time about Soviet ice radar activities at Dome B. Apparently Soviet glaciologists had been studying Dome B for 19 years. Sasha informed me that he'd been there personally on three occasions.

Sasha explained that the deepest ice at Dome B was 2,800 m from a surface elevation of around 3,000 m. Ten kilometres west of Dome B, the ice depth plunged to 3,600 m. At the time, the

Soviets were aware of eight subglacial lakes in the region, three new, the largest three kilometres long. Apparently, a drilling balok was located over one of the lakes. Special subsurface echo detecting equipment was due to be delivered to Mirny from the Arctic in two years' time to support their studies. While chatting to Sasha I was cut off abruptly by Dmitriev, who seemed outraged by our discussion – because it involved work matters. He eyeballed us sternly and grumbled, 'This is thoroughly improper!' then promptly switched the subject to … nude sunbathing.

I returned to Dom Geophisiki at 1am and discovered a separate party in my neighbour's room (No. 4). Naturally, I felt obliged to join in! The group included another Sasha, along with two Valodyas, Vassily and Ura. Our antics ensured all other residents remained awake, although brotherly comradeship tempered hard feelings the following day. Our dialogue was friendly, a little bit loud due to the alcohol, and rambling. Some of it involved discussion of our return voyage via Australia, epitomised below.

Hey Trev I am don't knowing English language very shortly, eez very small, only for skool. I was not been na skool wizzout leerning English yisik. Howz's suspression. How za vee may have za most useful frasa vee Australia. I am listened dis, by ze vay. Because I have zis ship … aargh shop … aargh ny ze prav. Trevol, so I will be correctly, I no so right remember ziss address. Etta vill be interesna for me to come back to ziss address. Ahhrr your also by ze vay in your language. By ze way I zink you as the same position. Etta expression … ooohh, ponymayesh. Yess, yes a Perrt, ahhrr how many kilometre of Fremantle. Eez by ze vay, my town where I lif has about 30 million. Wot! No … no … met, by ze way 30 tousand. Ooh nich-who-yar 300,000, Ny eta very small town where I live tolka. Yeeyaw znayesh Ron and absolutna also no talk wiz big speed indeed. But I am understanding all pochemu on sayd very fastly … no slowly. So Tref can you say for me what means, etcetera.

Monday 9 April 1984:

I arrived at the banya at 8am to find hot water unavailable. Didn't matter … I couldn't tell the difference anyway. I was sober, I thought, and hungry. I had no sleep the previous night and had missed breakfast. When I eventually reached the mess for lunch, my stomach turned – rubbery liver and spud again. Instead, I gulped down two bowls of soup.

I attempted an afternoon nap, but was interrupted by important priorities – vodka with Sasha, Valodya and Ura. At 6:15pm, Serdyukov, the outgoing OIC, presented a briefing to departing personnel to clarify the goods allowed to be returned to Russia. *Hopefully the talk doesn't apply to me*, I thought. My bags were fully packed and ready. I was keen to go home.

CHAPTER 7

Return to Australia

YOPZO YONTA

On my return, I have a thousand questions to ask.

Tuesday 10 April 1984:
Departing expeditioners waited on knife edge. We waited. We waited, and we waited for confirmation of departure details.

At 10am I dashed outside for fresh air. By chance, I caught sight of the *Kapitan Gotsky* emerging on the horizon. It was heading this way. Yahoo! What a thrill, given the obvious uncertainties. I stood and watched. I grinned as the *Gotsky* started to turn, and turn, which I found interesting at first, albeit unsettling. A few minutes went by, and it continued turning. My smile dissolved when I realised this was actually a U-turn. I watched, gobsmacked, as the *Gotsky* headed back out to sea! I spent the day waiting for an official explanation, or simply an update. Nothing. I'm sure others were confused as well. Desperately bored and unable to read, I sat on my bed and stared at my bags for hours on end. I paced up and down the corridor. Every now and then I glanced out the window to check for signs of activity, or change.

Dinner consisted of 'steak', potato and cabbage, which I swallowed gluttonously after rejecting similar offerings last night. At

6:30pm a short announcement came crackling over the loudspeaker: 'We will board tomorrow.' But something didn't smell right. The post-dinner movie was a Russian thriller resembling the 1970s movie *Airport*. The plot involved the personal intrigue of an aircrew, in-flight emergencies and sexual liaisons.

Wednesday 11 April 1984:

We waited all day without a further update. Calm skies precluded weather becoming a convenient excuse for the delay. Oleg informed me face to face 'departure planning revised again. We will not board Baikal immediately. We board Gotsky initially, then transfer at sea. Currently Baikal is in open water near the sea ice edge.'

This news signalled a dramatic and worrying change. To occupy time, I accepted an invitation from 'Nachanik' (means head of, or chief) Lorne, who invited me to inspect the powerhouse. He seemed surprised when I actually showed up, but nevertheless welcomed me warmly with a hug. Lorne was a generous host. On arrival, he scurried off to address first priorities: vodka and bread. 'Before looking at machinery,' he said, 'is necessary to take drink, vodka followed by tea, then … tour.'

The main powerhouse contained four generators with an individual output of 320 kW: one unit was functional, one unit under repair, two others on standby. The 'emergency' powerhouse consisted of a compact 500 kW army unit, recently installed in response to lessons learned from the '82 Vostok fire. Mirny's 'emergency' powerhouse was the first of its kind in the 27-year history of the station. I also learned about the tragic 1960 fire at Mirny that claimed the lives of eight victims, who now lie buried on Buromskiy Island, several kilometres to the north. Their gravesite is now a historic site, designated by the Antarctic Treaty Secretariat. The 1960 fire made little impression on me at the time, until I read about the detail years later. The fire risk was realised with another devastating event at

Mirny in 2020, which severely damaged the station but didn't result in fatalities. Fire is a terrifying risk in Antarctica. Once started, it can be difficult if not impossible to extinguish. Antarctic air is dry, materials are brittle, water is difficult to reticulate and fierce winds inflame combustion like a blacksmith's bellows.

During the early hours one day in 1960, one of the Mirny power station engineers noticed a failure in the electrical distribution system and traced it to the workplace and residence of meteorology section members. The engineer rang and woke the chief of section who calmly confirmed his bedroom light was out, that he could smell smoke, and that he would investigate immediately and come back. Then the phone went dead. The power station engineer called his supervisor, who together with others rushed to the affected building through darkness, snow drifts and winds. A fire alarm activated the entire base who turned up to fight the blaze using trucks, fire extinguishers and shovels. Fierce wind knocked men off their feet and fanned the flames, allowing the fire to remain out of control for hours. Several of the deceased suffocated under their bunks. One badly burned body was found part-way down a subsurface tunnel. He may have lost his life running through flames while attempting to escape. The cause of the 1960 fire at Mirny was never determined. It was one of the worst loss-of-life events in Antarctic history until shamefully eclipsed by Air New Zealand tourist Flight 901, which crashed into the side of Mt Erebus on 28 November 1979, killing all 237 passengers and 20 crew.

Even closer to the bone, I learned that the balok we used for the traverse to Dome C in 1983/84 was totally destroyed by fire the year after us (84/85) at a location close to Pionerskaya. The 84/85 traverse was heading for the last time to Dome C and planned to complete the removal of all ARMS. However, once the balok was destroyed, the traverse team necessarily and immediately returned to Mirny without accomplishing any science activities. The last and final traverse to Dome C was therefore postponed till the following year (85/86).

Back at Mirny, my guided tour of the powerhouse finished at 5pm. Lorne shuffled off again, this time mumbling about a present, while I continued chatting to the mechanics. On his return he thrust a balalaika at me, insisting I accept it, even though as I explained, 'I can't play a guitar'. 'But this … is gift,' he said, followed by a short recital to prove its worth as a musical instrument.

As I walked back to my room, the *Gotsky* had returned and was visible out to sea. At 8pm I received a call from Vlad, who requested I assemble my bags and equipment immediately and 'place them outside the main entrance to Dom Geophisiki, ready for collection'. Shortly after, the official update advised the suspension of loading activity until the following morning. 'What!?' A further announcement during the evening advised, 'Breakfast will be at 6am. First boat depart *Gotsky* at 7:30am.' My gear therefore spent a very cold night outside. Boarding arrangements were no doubt difficult to coordinate, but for departing expeditioners they were even more difficult to follow.

Thursday 12 April 1984:

By 10am, still no action. I peeked outside to observe a complete absence of embarkation activity. I couldn't help noticing something else: our resupply ship had disappeared again!

Later in the morning, departure details changed … again. The process appeared to be unravelling. Official updates became less frequent, overtaken by speculation and rumour. The reason for the delay appeared to be worsening pack ice in the local area. The pre-departure briefing held one week earlier had led us to expect the simultaneous arrival of two ships: the passenger vessel *MV Baikal*, on which I would return to Australia, and the ice-strengthened resupply cargo vessel *Kapitan Gotsky*.

I mistakenly imagined the *Baikal* would be a little red ship like *Nella Dan*, and therefore was surprised to discover it had a white hull, characteristic of a cruise ship – because, in fact, it was a cruise ship! The *Baikal*, I was reliably informed, normally ferried tourists from Nakhodka, a port city in Russia, to and from Yokohama in Japan during the northern summer. In Antarctica, the *Baikal*'s white hull presented to me the image of a speeding iceberg. Allegedly, this was the captain's first foray into Antarctic waters. The *Gotsky*, on the other hand, was a full-blown ice-strengthened supply ship that normally toured Soviet Antarctic stations to supply provisions and equipment independently from passenger operations.

Our departure in April was extremely late in the 'voyage' season. We were now within the period when 'fast ice'* could be expected. From what I understood, the *Gotsky* was re-routed from regular duties to specifically lead *Baikal* through the pack ice into Mirny. According to the rumour mill, the *Baikal* disappeared after arriving at Mirny because the captain became concerned for the safety of both his ship and passengers. Apparently, the captain realised his ship (with a passenger capacity of 262) was not safe amongst ice floes and had made a snap decision to return to the safety of open seas. And who could blame him? The *Gotsky* meanwhile steamed 10 km down the coast to the west, finding sanctuary from wind and fast ice by nudging into the base of towering ice cliffs. Our escape from Mirny was looking less and less likely by the hour. Outcomes could have swung either way. Nervous and unhappy about the possibility of being held over, an unsettling thought flashed through my mind. On one hand I reasoned, I would most likely become fluent in Russian if I stayed for the year. On the other hand... it might cost me my marriage.

I had sacrificed our first wedding anniversary located in a nondescript site on the Antarctic plateau, unable to contact Kerry who was clueless about my wellbeing and specific location. I had missed our first Christmas and first New Year's Eve as a married couple. I wasn't home for my 30th birthday, which occurred just after the traverse started. I wasn't home for Kerry's 26th birthday in February. Now it looked like I would be missing our first Easter together. If held over for the approaching winter, I would most likely be idle for six to eight months, with little professional activity possible.

Our situation changed dramatically during the late afternoon. I received an official update by word of mouth: 'Departing passengers must take personal bags only, and wait at the loading area at the base of rocky cliffs near diesel workshop.' A short time later, a flotilla of covered lifeboats began arriving from the *Gotsky*. Hopping from one foot to another to fend off shivering cold, dozens of us waited patiently while our bags were loaded. My JMRs, plus boxes of scientific gear and personal bags, were hurled unceremoniously into the boats. Then we jumped in like stampeding elephants, trampling across bags to huddle for warmth. Loading manifests and paperwork were totally absent – the scene reminiscent of a wartime evacuation.

We departed in the late afternoon as temperatures plummeted: the pervading mood apprehensive. No-one knew what to expect, nor the location of where we were headed. The lifeboat cabin was small. It offered precious little protection from the biting wind. Each boat was loaded and pushed off amid discordant shouting. The individual boats were held off momentarily until all boats were loaded, then they rallied together before setting off as a flotilla to chug down the coast for 50 minutes. Our trajectory hugged the base of towering ice cliffs, which provided merciful protection from the katabatic* wind high above. The stunning views attracted little interest from passengers, apart from an occasional glance. Our heads remained bowed to stave off the effects of chilling cold.

Eventually, our 'fun ride' ended as we pulled alongside the monstrous hull of the *Kapitan Gotsky*. Drift snow wafted over the lip of the ice cliffs above. Frigid air tumbled down the cliff face to form thick fog which spilled out and dispersed across the sea ice. Thankfully, the surrounding seas were calm, levelled by the damping effects of ice floes. Light winds whistled eerily through the ship's rails and rigging. The surreal ambience of our surroundings felt more like a movie set than reality.

First, we bundled personal gear into cargo nets for hoisting aboard using the ship's davit crane. Sailors on the foredeck handled the loads with haste rather than finesse. Time was of the essence. I crossed my fingers and hoped no items of mine would break or go astray. With the bags transferred, we followed by clambering out of the lifeboats to stand on a pallet in the same cargo net. Then, after being told to hang on, we were hoisted aboard like sacks of potatoes. I located and consolidated my gear, most of it dumped in a pile like soil from a tip truck. I ticked off a mental checklist: three soft bags tick, six crates tick, two JMR instrument cases, tick, various duffel bags tick, tick, tick. The only significant damage seemed to be a smashed protective case for JMR-1. The instrument itself was unscathed. I reasoned, 'No problem, the carry case just paid for itself!' In any event, I knew both instruments required a complete overhaul on return to Australia. My primary concern was ensuring these expensive instruments were not lost overboard.

With boarding concluded I started asking around … 'Where is the *Baikal*?' 'Not too far away', came the typical reply. Apparently, *MV Baikal* was manoeuvring at the outer limits of the sea ice where the pack was more dispersed. The next update informed us of *Baikal*'s relocation to a position 74 nautical miles from Mirny. This meant almost certainly that we'd spend our first night on the *Gotsky*, most likely slumped on a chair in the lounge, or on the floor of the mess, or perhaps leaning against a wall in a corridor. With crew numbers larger than usual, and now flooded with interlopers from Mirny, the *Gotsky* was thoroughly overcrowded, with absolutely no spare cabins or bunks.

Vlad and I were fortunate to be offered the lounge area in the chief engineer's suite, made available to us until the *Gotsky* rendezvoused with *Baikal* in the coming hours or days. We shared a long couch sleeping toe to toe. Remaining fully clothed, I grabbed a blanket and the chief engineer's heavy overcoat for additional warmth. It was absolutely soooooo ... bloody ... cold. Sleeping was extremely difficult. Apparently, Vlad got up at 4am, unable to sleep. I, meanwhile, lay there shivering until 8am, both of us chilled to the bone by the dreadful experience.

After wolfing down breakfast, most expeditioners proceeded outside to assess the situation and discovered the *Gotsky* hopelessly trapped in the sea ice. Tabular icebergs* threatened on both sides. We had barely moved overnight. The spectacular ice cliffs under which *Gotsky* anchored until we arrived remained clearly visible just kilometres away. Our hapless progress was difficult to believe given the thundering noises throughout the night – thrusting engines and crunching, crashing, finger-nail screeching, hull-clanging scraping noises from lumpy, floating ice banging against the steel hull. Fortunately, the news from *Baikal* was positive. Apparently, it had dodged entrapment and was waiting for us now, 50 nautical miles to our north. Personally, I hoped a blizzard might generate a polynya* as a means to exit the coastal pack. This didn't eventuate, and perhaps for the best, because otherwise I would have missed an eye-popping spectacle of derring-do Soviet escape artistry.

Friday 13 April 1984:

Unable to proceed forwards or backwards, we remained stationary for the entire day despite various methods of attempted escape. The first involved driving a pole abeam of the stern, then winching the ship backwards onto ice floes, hoping to crack the ice floe with the ship's deadweight. It didn't work.

The second method involved smashing holes manually into the ice to weaken it. The ship would ram the weakened area to try to create cracks. That didn't work either. Instead, the entrapment became tighter. The team regrouped to agree on a third strategy, a classic technique used by the earliest polar explorers involving a V-slot sawed manually in the ice, commencing from the bow. The idea aimed to open up a wedge and give the ship wriggle room to ram the floes more effectively. Excavated by the ship's crew and assisted by expeditioners, this was heavy, labour-intensive work. Dozens of cheery men with saws, crowbars, drills and shovels worked in small teams spread out across the surface to the rear of the ship. Their efforts continued through the day and into evening as daylight dimmed. After dinner, work recommenced under floodlight and continued until the ship finally proved it could wriggle, ever so slightly, the feat celebrated loudly by a rousing cheer – 'Hurrah! Hurrah!'

During our time onboard, half of the passengers dined in the officers' mess. The other half dined in the crew's mess. I hoped for improved meal quality, but found meals to be exactly the same quality as at Mirny. The standard dish consisted of meat with buckwheat, or variations thereof, such as buckwheat with meat. The 'high Soviet' passenger lounge was adorned with posters of Supreme Soviet members, supplemented with political paraphernalia, recent magazines, motivational posters and tatty back-issues of the Moscow daily newspaper, *Pravda*, spread over numerous side tables.

My improved Russian language facilitated interaction with a larger group of expeditioners, most of whom I hadn't met previously. Many were eager to practice conversational English with me, listening or conversing in a combination of English and Russian, mostly about life in Australia. Although heart-warming and enjoyable, and better than being ignored, the experience demanded intense concentration. I still found conversation in Russian to be challenging despite months of practice and immersion. Vlad requested I present a talk to the crew and passengers. I was reluctant for two reasons. I felt my language was inadequate, plus I lacked slides or pictures.

Vlad offered to help as a translator but we couldn't find a projector, so we didn't proceed.

Saturday 14 April 1984:

The chief engineer invited Vlad and me to join him for a tour of the ship. We started at the bridge where, to my surprise, I discovered an American-made Magnavox MX1102 satellite navigation unit. Apparently, the Magnavox units were installed five years earlier (in 1979) across the entire fleet of Soviet Antarctic resupply vessels. The Soviet Union had their own proprietary sat nav system at the time, but as the chief explained, equivalent Soviet units were large and clumsy. They much preferred the American technology for civilian applications. My other early impression involved the huge size of the bridge. Large, cold, draughty and sterile; altogether different from the cosy warm atmosphere on the bridge of Nella Dan.

Our second stop was a quick peek into the radio shack, being worked at the time by three operators. Next, we headed to the engine room where the ruckus was predictably ear-shattering. We followed the chief down steep ladders between machinery and boilers, mostly without speaking, while he pointed at things and I nodded. The chief used body language to communicate as the situation demanded, then we moved through a door into the quiet sanctuary of the engine's control room where he resumed the verbal narrative without a pause. Vlad threw in a few English phrases to fill in obvious gaps in my understanding. 'Unlike American ships …' the chief explained, 'Soviet Antarctic vessels are driven by electric engines.' 'Electric drive has advantage!' he exclaimed, 'greater speed control, ease of forward and reverse modes without requiring gearbox, greater torque at low revs, and safety.'

According to the chief, electric drive offered flexibility not possible with mechanical drive systems, particularly in Antarctica, if one of the four blade propellers happened to strike ice. He pointed to the control panels applicable to each of the nine diesel engines. 'These provide source energy for onboard generator.' I nodded wisely. 'The engine compartment also contains a desalination plant with freshwater production capacity of 7.8 tonnes per day.' Belonging to the Far East Shipping Company and aged 18 years with an expected service life of 25 years, *Kapitan Gotsky* combined ballast tanks in both the bow and stern to break ice by rocking, a system most effective when the ship was fully laden.

The *Gotsky* itinerary entailed a return to home port in Vladivostok by September. The normal operating crew of 51 had swelled currently to 86, the larger numbers in part due to the presence of three helicopter crews to support loading and unloading operations, plus a team of three hardhat divers who inspected the hull periodically. The crew also included six females: a doctor, cook, baker, stewardess and two crewmembers associated with the meals service. The vessel's unusual V-shaped stern contained a huge inbuilt winch to allow sister ships to be dragged in at close quarters for towing through pack ice.

By midday, we had the *Baikal* in sight, positioned 90 nautical miles from Mirny. As the two ships drew near, the *Baikal* positioned itself behind the *Gotsky*, an arrangement that continued for the remainder of the day. The captains of both ships searched for a polynya, or a sufficiently large patch of open water, to allow both ships to pull alongside and thus facilitate the passenger transfer, hopefully before nightfall. In the meantime, the weather gradually deteriorated. The forecast suggested imminent gale-force winds, which posed a serious threat to the safety of both ships and, of course, to all onboard. The *Baikal* continued to follow closely in the wake of *Gotsky* as we navigated a jungle of ice floes, growlers, bergy bits and pack ice. Heavy ice on both sides continued to prevent the *Baikal* from pulling alongside.

At the first safe opportunity, the Baikal stopped dead in the water while the *Gotsky* continued on with a slow manoeuvre. Picking its way through jumbled channels and cracks in the ice, the *Gotsky* circled and repositioned itself behind the *Baikal*. Next, it nudged its way forward slowly and carefully to pull alongside, but slightly away from the *Baikal*. To complete the quasi-docking process, both vessels inched forward together to touch delicately at the bow only in a V formation. This entire process consumed many hours, mostly in complete darkness. By midnight, both ships were safely nestled together. Out on the foredecks, crew activity was noisy, theatrical and very James Bond – totally thrilling! The wind howled! It was pitch black. Swirling snow blustered over the decks, illuminated by intense floodlights. Out in the middle of the Southern Ocean on the darkest of nights, the atmosphere reminded me of a favourite Disney pirate movie, *The Mooncussers*. Fall protection nets thrown between the ships were secured on both sides, followed by the installation of a temporary walkway fashioned from timber planks with rope handrails several metres long. Both crews worked seamlessly and tirelessly as transfer preparations advanced. Fortunately, the weather remained calm.

Our next operation, the transfer itself, occurred informally and quickly with no briefings, no safety gear other than a catch net, and no rollcall. Anonymous voices from invisible sailors bellowed out garbled instructions and advice (in Russian). Scrambling across the walkway, nervously clutching rope handrails, each man scurried like a performing rat laden with personal baggage and boxes of all types and sizes.

I had too many items to manage alone, but I was offered assistance by traverse colleagues including Sergey (magnetologist) and his wintering workmates from Molodezhnaya. My gear transferred successfully without incident, and the entire process occurred without incident – a remarkable outcome in the circumstances. Once onboard the *Baikal*, I gathered my chattels, hunted down my allocated cabin, packed away my kitbags and changed clothes immediately.

Parties ignited spontaneously in various cabins. Porthole curtains were drawn as vodka flowed. Typically, seven or eight people were crammed into a cabin for two. I staggered through several celebrations before finding my bunk again at 5am. Needless to say, a huge hangover meant I slept through the entire day.

Sunday 15 April 1984:

When I saw the Baikal for the first time, I thought it the most unlikely vessel to find in Antarctica. My trepidation evaporated as we emerged into the open ocean. The Baikal quickly demonstrated its credentials for returning expeditioners.

Cruise ship living areas and showy, ornamental cabin appointments contrasted favourably with the drab décor of the *Kapitan Gotsky*. *Baikal* crew were almost exclusively female, facilitating cabaret performances after the evening meal. Eager expeditioners seated around circular drinks tables lapped it up. This Antarctic return voyage was unlike anything I could have imagined. Yet again I was struck by comparisons with *Nella Dan*. *Nella* did not offer dancing girls, but the meals were tasty, diverse and abundant. Meals on *Nella Dan* were delivered with exceptional service in a cosy dining room featuring exquisite brass and timber fittings, and beautifully laundered linen tablecloths. The meals on the *Baikal* were like meals on the *Gotsky*, which were similar to meals at the station. Enough said! But, as a cruise ship, it offered proper bathrooms and comfortable, warm cabins. Suddenly, Levi jeans, Wrangler shirts, sneakers, leather jackets and a plethora of blue tracksuits replaced the windproof parkas to which I'd become accustomed. Suddenly, the corridors and cabins were filled with smells of eau de cologne. Suddenly, clean-shaven, smartly dressed men were strutting their stuff in the corridors and on the poop deck.

However, the downside was also sudden. I couldn't recognise colleagues due to the absence of superficial characteristics on which I'd previously relied, such as a scruffy beard, a quirky balaclava, or a torn parka. For the next few days, I relied on tone of voice and eyes to recognise and reconnect with individuals with whom I thought I was acquainted.

The remainder of my voyage home was unremarkable. The *Baikal* docked in Fremantle at 12 noon on 21 April 1984. My welcome-home party consisted of Perth-based relatives and one AAD public relations representative who had travelled from Hobart to coordinate my disembarkation and plane ticket home. Shortly after arrival I was interviewed by *The West Australian* newspaper and Channel Nine News WA and featured in a newspaper and evening news segment. The following day I invited a group of traverse comrades to lunch with me at a café in Fremantle. My AAD colleague also arranged the hire of a mini-bus and we took several groups on an impromptu sightseeing tour of Fremantle before I left the ship formally and flew home to Melbourne.

During my red-eye special from Perth to Melbourne I had one final celebrity moment. While seated in the aisle seat in the last row, an air hostess sidled up to me with the morning paper, *The West Australian*, opened at an interior page featuring the pictorial article about my arrival. 'Is that you?' she said, pointing at the article. I was still wearing the same jumper, a green shawl-neck garment hand-knitted by Kerry. My hair, dishevelled and uncut for five months, was clearly recognisable. I was clean at least, and as far as I could tell, didn't smell. The newspaper picture showed me hanging out of a cabin porthole, one arm thrust in the air holding my gifted balalaika. Fortunately, my celebrity came with entitlements. I asked for a second meal and got it! Looking back at photographs of the time, I was so thin the hostess must have thought she was saving me from starvation. Kerry was waiting for me at the gate at Melbourne Airport. Two hours later we were back at our home in Mt Eliza.

CHAPTER 8

Epilogue

YAANF

How are you darling.

The Soviet expedition was a once-in-a-lifetime experience, but not the end of my Antarctic adventures. My employment continued with the Glaciology Section through to early 1986 and then transferred to the Special Projects Group of AAD. In July Kerry and I, along with three-month-old baby Ben, relocated to Head Office in Kingston, Tasmania. I bought a trailer and loaded it with baby gear, clothing and personal effects. We crossed Bass Strait on the *Spirit of Tasmania*, then drove from Devonport to Hobart.

For the first few months we lived in the 'Antarctic Lodge' adjacent to Little Beach in Beach Road, Sandy Bay, now infamous as the location where Dark Mofo swimmers gather annually for a midwinter nudie-romp in the Derwent River. Most residents were single male expeditioners. I, together with my single colleagues, travelled to and from work at the AAD Head Office Kingston in a government-supplied minibus.

A quaint feature of our two-bedroom 'flat' (we didn't call them apartments in those days) at Antarctic Lodge, apart from the tiny rooms and even tinier spaces, was the gold Telecom[11] Australia pay-

---

11. Telecom Australia changed its name to Telstra in 1995.

phone. Every flat at the Antarctic Lodge had one. The manager came around once a month to unlock and empty the coin tray. We spent $70 every month and didn't have a credit card. Kerry would buy back the coins with notes so that we had enough change for the following month. Our calls were for local and long distance (known as Subscriber Trunk Dialling / STD) only. We never called overseas and nobody ever rang us. Ours was a 'phone box number' rather than a landline number. For some reason, both friends and relatives seemed unwilling to ring us, or even try to ring us.

In the mid-1980s, local phone calls typically cost 25 cents. Most of our calls were 'long distance' and charged by the minute. The only free call '1194', permitted a caller to check the local time – 'At the third stroke it will be 3:33 and forty seconds, precisely ... beep, beep, beep' – a service that ended in 2019. As a result of the discipline forced on us by the 'gold phone', Kerry and I fell into an ongoing habit of calling family members only after 7pm and before 10pm, when phone rates were cheaper. Handheld mobile phones the size and weight of a brick were introduced to Australia in 1987. The Internet was only available to the public in Australia in the 1990s.

Our residency at Antarctic Lodge ended abruptly one day during a horrific summer storm. The day was unusually hot for Hobart, with a top temperature of 34°C. Kerry (full name Kerry-Lynne)[12] was at the shops during the morning and experienced an unusual migraine, perhaps an omen. She returned to the flat in the late morning just as the thunderstorms hit. A torrential downpour soon exposed blocked drains. Within minutes, both the gardens and carparks were underwater, with rain continuing unabated as the water levels rose. Kerry called me on the landline to ask me to come home. I was with work colleagues through the entire event and didn't receive her message directly. Well, in truth, I was 'at lunch' at the Kingston Hotel with work colleagues and didn't appreciate the seriousness of the situation.

---

12. Celtic for 'dark lake'.

Kerry sat our six-month-old baby Ben on the bed while she lifted bags and objects from the floor and placed them on kitchen benches and on the top of beds. Eventually, rising water forced her out of the flat. We lost several minor belongings that lay hidden at the back of the kitchen cupboards. More seriously, Kerry forgot about my remote-control glider stored under one of the beds. It was ruined! Both our passports, which had been stored in a bedside table, were also damaged.

During the storm, the manager of Antarctic Lodge offered Kerry access to a recently cleaned and vacant room on the first floor. Then part of the ceiling in the upstairs flat also collapsed. I arrived home to an epic 'oh shit' moment. The water penetrated all ground-floor units and finished halfway up the side of several vehicles, including our old unbustable Toyota Corona. Several expeditioners lost Bang and Olufsen (B&O) hi-fi equipment. In those days expeditioners would purchase expensive B&O systems duty-free from Denmark by ordering and receiving delivery through the Lauritzen Line[13] purser.[14] Immediately after the flood, single men living in other units were relocated to hotel rooms. Unfortunately, my parents were visiting from Victoria at the time and away from the flat on a drive around other parts of the island. We had no way of contacting them and no other obvious place to live in the meantime. So, for two nights we slept in the crudely washed out but still muddied and very smelly flat.

Fortunately, a female work colleague took pity and offered us her brand-new villa as a rental. She went off to live elsewhere with her boyfriend and we re-located to the emerging riverside suburb of Blackmans Bay. For several weeks while our car was being repaired, I walked to and from work – four kilometres into Kingston and four

---

13. The owners of *Nella Dan*.

14. The purser (or treasurer or bursar) on a ship is charged with keeping accounts and the distribution of money.

kilometres back. Kerry purchased groceries each day from a local shop, only small amounts capable of being carried in the pusher with Ben. Occasionally, Kerry would take a bus trip into Hobart with Ben to visit a larger shopping centre or the doctor.

At Head Office I worked on several projects: the first commenced while we still lived in Melbourne – a 'Feasibility Study on the use of helicopters to support glaciology investigations on the Lambert Glacier'.[15] One exciting aspect of this assignment was the opportunity to fly all over Melbourne as an observer in the Victoria Police Bell 412SP – the rotary aircraft shortlisted for our Antarctic logistics program. Another achievement was the publication of an AAD Research Note (Hamley, Morgan, Thwaites & Gao, 1986) documenting the site on Law Dome best suited for a 'deep ice core mechanical drill project'. One of my co-authors, Gao, was one of several Chinese glaciologists from the Lanzhou Institute, China. Gao was invited by the AAD to work and study with the glaciology section during the 1980s at a time when cooperation between the two countries was extremely positive. The Chinese were in the early days of becoming interested in Antarctica through the lens of science. They have since constructed five Antarctic research stations.

I finalised and published a paper on iceberg dissolution (Hamley & Budd, 1986), one of the first to analyse iceberg data and draw meaningful conclusions from years of shipboard observations. Recently, I discovered my work – which was supervised and co-authored by the late Professor Bill Budd – acknowledged in a paper by Orheim et al. (2022). In 1986 I worked under the leadership of a former naval commander. I assisted the executive team developing specifications for the now-retired Australian icebreaker *Aurora Australis* – constructed and launched in 1989 at Carrington Slipways, Newcastle for P&O Australia.

---

15. The Lambert Glacier is the world's largest and feeds into the Amery Iceshelf.

One of the most satisfying aspects of my career as a glaciologist was the lifelong friendship Kerry and I formed with Vlad and his wife Natasha. In 1994, (well after leaving my employment with the Antarctic Division) Vlad and his colleague Boris from the IZMIRAN institute in Moscow reached out to contact me while attending the ANARE research group in Tasmania. Kerry and I had recently relocated to Mt Eliza after moving and living all over Australia with work commitments. Amazingly, we still had the same landline telephone number.

At the time Vlad rang, I was on a work trip in Kalgoorlie Western Australia. Kerry answered the phone. 'Hello ...' said a strange voice. 'I am lookink (sic) for Doctor Hamley.' Kerry was alert to the accent and realised immediately who it was, but nevertheless responded cautiously. 'I think you may have the wrong number. Who's calling?' 'Ah. My name is Professor Vladimir ...' 'Oh ...' said Kerry, 'I know who you are ... Trevor will be back home at the weekend.' Vlad left a contact number and I returned the call as soon as I arrived home. We invited Vlad and Boris to stay for the weekend.

After collecting Vlad and Boris at Melbourne airport, we drove to our home in Mt Eliza with a detour for afternoon tea at the residence of Boris and Vlad's former Moscow colleague, geophysicist Professor Valery Troitskaya. Kerry, meanwhile, invited nearby friends Marc and Judith over for dinner. They brought a Japanese exchange student who was boarding with them at the time. Judith is Lithuanian by descent and a language teacher of both French and Japanese. Dinner turned into a multi-language exchange involving continual translation between English, Russian and Japanese – a real hoot, one of those evenings you never forget.

Boris looked and dressed like the archetypical KGB agent. He wore a waist-length leather coat – I think it was grafted on. He had straggly, balding hair with a craggy facial profile and a fag always hanging out of his mouth. He was a lovely man who could understand English, but not as well as Vlad. Boris chain-smoked black cigarellos. He asked Kerry politely at one stage, 'Is okay to smoke inside house?', expecting polite affirmation, but was miffed when Kerry ordered him outside. It was a cold night and our open fire was raging. 'Oh, Australian women ... werry bossy,' said Boris. Vlad just laughed. Boris also inquired innocently, 'How many families live in zis house?'

The following day I took Vlad and Boris for a scenic drive. While passing through the Melbourne CBD I stopped opportunistically to show them the stock exchange. The ASX had recently moved to new premises at 530 Collins St. It was a computerised facility with no trading floor, unlike contemporary US stock exchanges of the day. The ASX was the premier financial institution in the city, and a prominent part of Melbourne history having grown out of the former Melbourne Stock Exchange (Australia's first stock exchange) that commenced trading in 1859. From the street, the only physical evidence of goings-on inside was an atrium with large, illuminated displays quoting stock prices. But it was truly a stop of interest to my visitors. This was the era of Boris Yeltsin. Economically speaking, the USSR was in a bit of a state. When we returned to the car, I had a parking ticket. 'No problem,' said Vlad and Boris. They disappeared for a long period to supposedly make a phone call from a public telephone. After they left town, I discovered the fine was paid, but I never did figure out how this occurred. Vlad swears to this day he had nothing to do with it. KGB, maybe?

At the time (1994), our eldest son Ben was in grade three at Kunyung Primary School in Mt Eliza, Victoria. Our younger son Tom was at Mt Eliza Pre-school. Vlad had a son at school in Moscow of a similar age to Ben and was curious about the Australian school system. He asked many questions and showed interest in seeing Ben's school. I was involved with the parents committee and knew the principal so I requested permission for our visitors to peek into

Ben's classroom during school hours. The children were learning about climate at the time.

In no time at all, Vlad and Boris had the kids gathered in a circle on the floor listening to Vlad explain their work as scientists in the context of the interplanetary magnetic field, for example how planets rotate around the sun and cause ripples like water flowing in a river when they pass by the Earth. The children were transfixed and asked a flood of intelligent questions. I'm sure this was the genesis of several future science careers. The principal was less sure until he saw Vlad and Boris front and centre on a television news segment the following evening with the banner headline 'Russian scientists visit Melbourne'.

CHAPTER 9

Reflection

YOOZK

In reply to your telex my answer is no.

Publication of this book coincides with the 40th anniversary of my participation in the Soviet Antarctic Expedition, and 41 years of marriage to Kerry. Kerry and I have, in the meantime, completed mainstream professional careers, moved house numerous times around Australia and overseas, and raised a family of two sons. We currently have several grandchildren, and all the while have maintained close contact and friendship with Vlad and Natasha who emigrated to the US and for more than 30 years now, proudly called themselves Russian Americans.

Kerry inspired me to write this book for the benefit of family – to share details of my unique experience – and to possibly inspire future generations. Kerry's touchpoint with my adventure was different from mine. While I was away, Kerry received feedback that has remained with her ever since. When I departed, Kerry feared that I may never return, a fear not entirely unfounded. My thirst for adventure (with apologies to Roald Amundsen) provided a perceived immunity to danger as it does for most young people and I beetled on. Yet, had any one of several events taken a turn for the worse,

Kerry may well have been widowed at 25. I may have been critically injured by the quad bike at Mawson or disappeared into what turned out to be an imagined crevasse, not to speak of our mechanical emergencies, fire and medical catastrophes during the traverse. Kerry kept a diary while I was away but disposed of it shortly after I returned. She also took Vlad and Boris to visit our son Tom's preschool (after they visited Ben's classroom) where she was President at the time. In subsequent years (2006 onwards), Kerry continued to introduce Vlad to senior high school physics students using early internet messaging systems to allow students to interact with a 'real' science practitioner.

Several Australian glaciologists participated in the Dome C traverse before me. Several Australians visited Vostok before me. Few encountered the calamity I experienced. To the best of my knowledge, no other field party in the history of Antarctic exploration has removed an appendix in the field.

Despite adversity, the glaciology program collected useful data and achieved expectations. I finalised the remeasurement of 16 ice movement markers, including all nine 'priority 1' stations. Snow accumulation readings and snow samples were successfully gathered and onforwarded to Australian and international laboratories. The surface ice movement data provided ground-truth for computerised mass balance models being developed in Australia at the time. But did this work add value? Related Essay B – 'Glaciology and Climate Change' explains. Vlad successfully visited the Soviet ARMS, which included the deployment of one new station and one manual measurement of absolute values of the magnetic field.

The Mirny to Dome C traverse showcased the finest attributes of the *Antarctic Treaty*. We demonstrated how science can bridge political canyons and facilitate unlikely friendships, lifelong friendships. Russian men and women are very similar to Australians in terms of family values, educational aspirations, career ambitions, sporting and travel interests, innate sense of right and wrong, and religious and ethnic diversity.

My hope is for the *Antarctic Treaty* to continue in its current form. Antarctica is a sanctuary for unique and diverse wildlife and natural beauty. Increasing numbers of countries are establishing stations. Increasing numbers of tourists are flocking to Antarctica as the last frontier. I can't help wondering about the motivations, and the future of political manoeuvres that may occur after 2048 when any of the Treaty parties may call for a review. Field activities of the kind I experienced are a great pathway to peace in the region. They should be encouraged, including ongoing international coordination of conservation activities for fishing, whaling and tourism.

I encourage anyone who would like to do something to go out and do it. If you dream it, you can achieve it! Set a goal, then figure out how to get there. Being a scientist, for example, requires an enquiring mind much more than being top of the class in mathematics. Although it might seem like a daunting amount of work, or something that requires a lot of luck, you won't achieve goals unless you put yourself out there, including writing a book.

YITWE expeditions.

Acknowledgements

YINAC

Did not hear your message on Radio Australia

I could not have written this book without inspiration from my wife Kerry. Her encouragement and advice assisted me to maintain momentum and a high standard. I also thank my two sons Ben and Tom for their interest and encouragement.

A chance reconnection in Tasmania during 2022 with one of my earliest glaciology colleagues, Jo Jacka, resulted in my first external input on this project. As a former Chief Editor of the *Journal of Glaciology*, Jo was the first person apart from Kerry to read an early manuscript and offer improvement suggestions. I sincerely thank Jo for his encouragement and assistance.

Next, I sought the imprimatur of Vladimir Papitashvili, our traverse leader. This memoir describes a shared experience. Vlad's contribution goes beyond words. Vlad reviewed the manuscript and promptly provided feedback while working full-time for the National Science Foundation as Program Director of Science for the US South Pole station. I also acknowledge and pay tribute to our 1983/84 Soviet traverse colleagues with whom I have now lost contact. As a result of this memoir, I have rekindled the memory of our unbelievable experience together.

Numerous friends and acquaintances assisted me as advance readers, for which I am grateful. Thank you, Peter Keage, Jeff Wilson, Graham Stanley, Marina Marangos, Charles Gilks, Ellie Rath, Robyn Jaques, Paul Perrot, Celia Grenning, Verity Mansfield, Sue Abbey, Gill Booysen and Milt Booysen. I particularly thank Joan Meecham, whose thorough review identified ambiguities and omissions before I could burden others.

Information sources are cited where appropriate, but my writings on science are not peer-reviewed with the rigour of a paper published in a recognised scientific journal. Therefore, my commentary should not be relied on as scholarly work. Information not particularised by reference was gleaned from publicly available sources. My purpose is to entertain and stimulate informed discussion.

Thank you Brisbane Self Publishing Service: Kirsty Ogden and Rebecca Fletcher who steered me through the line editing and publication process.

Finally, I thank and acknowledge the Australian Antarctic Division and Soviet Arctic and Antarctic Research Institute in Leningrad for providing me with the opportunity to participate in the adventure of a lifetime.

RELATED ESSAYS

The Story of Dr Leonid Rogosov

In 1961 Dr Leonid Rogosov – the only doctor at the Russian Antarctic station, Novolazarevskaya – diagnosed himself with acute appendicitis. He realised he needed surgery to survive and understood the impossibility of evacuation. Dr Rogosov successfully removed his own appendix in an operation performed with local anaesthetic, untrained assistants, and for the most part without using gloves – to maximise the sense of touch. The operation occurred 60 years ago yet continues to intrigue those who hear about it for the first time. The story featured in a 1964 Soviet Antarctic Expedition Information Bulletin and separately, was an exhibit in the Museum of St Petersburg. Rogosov's story is well known within the Antarctic medical community and abdominal surgeons globally, but less well known in the West. His account shares similarities and touchpoints with our circumstances with Valentine G. Our patient's appendicectomy occurred in the field, also without general anaesthetic, by the light of incandescent globes and two handheld flashlights while lying on top of our dinner table, high on the Antarctic plateau.

In 2009, Rogosov's story was written-up in the *British Medical Journal* and subsequently covered in 2015 by the BBC World Service program *Witness*. In 2017 the US radio program *This American Life* discussed Rogosov's experience with two contemporary medical experts, one who had been a doctor at the US South Pole station Amundsen-Scott in 2012 – at the time of the radio program he was working for NASA caring for astronauts. The other medic had not heard about Rogosov's experience but had written about appendicectomies for textbooks and journals and performed the procedure many times. All marvelled at Rogosov's astonishing mental toughness, in particular the ability to assemble a team, instruct them on what to do, then concentrate and work effectively while suffering intense pain. The medical experts agreed that Rogosov's self-surgery was brave and audacious. His story lives on through his son Vasilev Rogosov (also a doctor) who wrote about the process in Rogosov & Bermel, 2009.

Following Rogosov's instructions, team members at Novolazarevskaya assembled an improvised operating theatre. Rogosov selected a meteorologist, mechanic and station director as assistants. He briefed them on how to inject the drugs and syringes that he prepared, and how to provide artificial ventilation. The meteorologist handed him instruments. The mechanic held the mirror and adjusted lighting from the table lamp. Rogosov requested the station director step in if nausea overcame either of the active assistants, and to instruct the team should he lose consciousness.

Rogosov injected himself with local anaesthetic, waited 15 minutes then made a 10 cm to 12 cm incision, moving his intestines out of the way and feeling for a firm 'sausage' – the appendix. After 30 to 40 minutes, he began taking breaks then removed the inflamed appendix, applied antibiotics in the peritoneal cavity and closed the wound. The operation lasted an hour and 45 minutes. Rogosov's temperature rose the day after the surgery, but two weeks of antibiotics eliminated all infection and Rogosov went back to work.

A BBC article (Lentati, 2015) described the operation citing comparisons made by the Soviet propoganda machine between Yuri Gagarin also 27 and the first man in space, and Rogosov's incredible survival story. Rogosov was awarded the Order of the Red Banner of Labour, which honoured great deeds and services to the Soviet state and society. His bravery was held up as a symbol to the rest of the world. Rogosov (like our Slava) shunned the publicity and went back to his hospital to resume his career.

Glaciology and Climate Change

Introduction

The Earth's rotational axis is tilted to the Earth's orbital plane around the sun by an angle of 23.5°. Thus, the Tropic of Cancer and Tropic of Capricorn are located at latitudes 23.5°N and 23.5°S respectively. Both the Arctic Circle and Antarctic Circle are defined as the latitude for the relevant pole, minus the tilt of the Earth. The Arctic Circle lies at latitude (90-23.5=) 66.5° north of the equator. The Antarctic Circle lies at latitude 66.5° south of the equator.

At the summer solstice,[16] a person located anywhere on the Antarctic Circle will observe the sun above the horizon for one full 24-hour period. On this day, the Earth's southern hemisphere is tilted to its greatest extent towards the sun. Observers further south than the Antarctic Circle will see the sun above the horizon for longer than a full day. Those at the Geographic South Pole experience non-stop daylight with the sun circling in the sky for a total of six months, from the southern autumnal equinox,[17] until the

---

16. The summer solstice is the longest day of the year, occurring around 21 or 22 December in the southern hemisphere.

17. The autumnal equinox is the day when the length of daylight and night are the same, occurring around 20 or 21 March in the southern hemisphere.

southern vernal equinox.[18] During this period, observers within the Arctic Circle experience the exact opposite. They do not see the sun.

The Earth is not a perfect sphere. It is an imperfect oblate spheroid or irregularly shaped ellipsoid. In other words, the Earth is egg-shaped, with the polar regions slightly flatter and the equator region slightly pudgier. The southern hemisphere bulges more than the northern hemisphere and is slightly bigger in surface area. Earth's spin is the reason polar areas are slightly flattened.

By definition, East Antarctica lies to the east of the prime meridian (longitude 0°) passing through Greenwich, England.

The effect of rising global air temperatures and increasing carbon dioxide levels have been widely researched and publicised over recent decades. Authorities have concluded that the area covered by sea ice in the Arctic at the end of summer has shrunk by around 40% since 1979. The decreasing Arctic minimum sea ice extent is concerning because sea ice reflects up to 80% of incoming sunlight, forming an insulating layer between the warm ocean and the cold atmosphere. Carbon dioxide absorbs wavelengths of thermal energy causing Earth's temperature to rise. It is a long-lived greenhouse gas responsible for two-thirds of the energy imbalance. Since 1880, the mean temperature of the Earth's surface is generally agreed by scientists to have risen by about 1.0°C.

Antarctica is totally surrounded by the Southern Ocean. In winter, the surface area of ice cover doubles due to the formation of Antarctic sea ice, of which 15% normally remains during the summer at a minimum. Therefore, the majority of Antarctic sea ice is one winter old and relatively thin, often one metre or less. The minimum and maximum extent of floating sea ice in both the Arctic and Antarctica is rarely the same from year to year.

---

18. The vernal equinox is the second day of the year when the length of daylight and night are the same, occurring around 22 or 23 September in the southern hemisphere.

After studying decades of sea ice data since the 1970s, scientists concluded:

- Arctic sea ice cover has generally decreased.
- Antarctic sea ice cover has generally increased – although the worryingly depleted sea ice cover in 2023 may have reversed that trend.
- Overall, the net global cover in sea ice extent has decreased.

Unravelling what this means practically speaking is not easy. Antarctic sea ice is highly variable on a yearly basis. After 30 years of gradual but uneven increase in average sea ice cover, 2014 proved to be the highest extent on record, followed by a precipitous decline in 2017 to the lowest minimum extent recorded in a study period of 40 years.

Whereas the causal link to decreasing Arctic sea ice is unambiguously attributed to climate change, it seems the behaviour of Antarctic sea ice is not so obvious. Antarctic sea ice extent may be related to natural variability. Many theories have been posed to explain the relationship: they include consideration of holes in the ozone layer, connections to the El Nino Southern Oscillation, and the presence of increased basal meltwater from Antarctic ice shelves.

The Mass Balance of the East Antarctic Ice Sheet

Several decades have passed since my expedition with the Soviets and the subsequent publication of my Master of Science (MSc) thesis. I couldn't help wondering whether my MSc remained relevant today. In 1987 I stated, amongst other things, 'The comparison between field measurements and calculated balance fluxes has shown the East Antarctic Ice Sheet, at present, is unlikely to be significantly out of balance (i.e. within +/- 10%).'

An ice sheet, by definition, is an ice field of more than 50,000 square kilometres. Like a glacier, an ice sheet forms through the accumulation of surface snow, increasing in thickness until it compacts to form ice, then deforms under its own weight, that is to flow, in the down-slope direction. Unlike a glacier, an ice sheet flows outward in all directions, moving slowly from the centre, then faster as the ice inexorably moves towards the coast.

Mass balance refers to the difference between an ice sheet's total snow input and total ice loss, achieved through the combined effects of melting, ablation or calving. If an ice sheet gains as much through snowfall as it loses through melting, ablation and calving from glaciers and icebergs, then it is said to be 'in balance'. If the output exceeds input, the ice sheet is described as losing mass (a negative mass balance). If the input snowfall is greater than the output, the ice sheet is described as gaining mass (a positive mass balance). Determining trends requires decades of accumulated observations, measurement and analyses.

In various places, the Antarctic ice is hundreds of thousands of years old, allowing glaciologists to determine past climate and past environmental history by sampling ice-cores. During the last ice age – prior to 15,000 years ago – most ice sheets were in the northern hemisphere. Today, the Earth's two major ice sheets (i.e. Antarctica and Greenland) contain 99% of the world's freshwater ice. The Antarctic Ice Sheet is eight times larger than the Greenland Ice Sheet and lies in the southern hemisphere. Greenland lies in the northern hemisphere and is around 2.16 million square kilometres in area of which 80%, or 1.7 million square kilometres, is covered by ice sheet.

According to Fretwell et al. (2013, p. 390), 'Antarctica:

- covers an area of 12.3 million square kilometres excluding ice shelves;
- contains 26.5 million cubic kilometres of ice (where a cubic kilometre of ice weighs approximately one metric gigaton, or one billion tons) excluding ice shelves.'

The speed of the surface ice flow is very slow in the centre of Antarctica. At Vostok, satellite doppler measurements reveal a computed surface velocity of 2.0 +/- 0.6 metres per annum, at an azimuth* of 139° True. Towards the coast, ice flow speeds up. The ice sheet thins and is channelled by features of the subsurface landmass to exit the coast through large outlet glaciers. Glacier tongues typically show speeds in the order of hundreds of metres per year. The higher ice flow speed is possible because the glacier is both sliding at the base and deforming internally.

My MSc suggested the East Antarctic Ice Sheet was in balance. It was an unsophisticated conclusion determined by comparing field measurements of surface ice velocity and snow accumulation for a chosen flow line in East Antarctica against the results of computer modelling for an assumed state of zero mass balance.

Since the 1980s glaciologists have been united about the state of mass balance for both West Antarctica and Greenland. Both regions are experiencing unambiguous and significant ice loss. Glaciologists are less united about the situation in East Antarctica, where the evidence is complex. Some studies suggest the East Antarctic Ice Sheet is growing or gaining mass, others suggest it is shrinking or losing mass. A scholarly paper from the NASA Goddard Space Centre by Zwally et al. (2015) caused controversy in the scientific community by suggesting the Antarctic icesheet mass is increasing. This conclusion was not consistent with a large body of previously published work, which led to concerns about the possibility of confusing policy makers and the general public, and the effect contrary conclusions may have on the climate change movement generally. Scambos and Shuman (2016) criticised the findings and methods of Zwally et al. in an open letter to the *Journal of Glaciology*. They challenged Zwally's method of calculating the surface height of the snow and tabulated independent assessments of surface elevation change to show different outcomes.

In rebuttal, Zwally et al. contended that the results and conclusions, when combined with evidence of accumulation increases that commenced 10,000 years ago, evidenced long-term thickening in East Antarctica, providing a continuing and small beneficial impact to the current rate of global sea-level rise. Zwally also rebutted criticisms of technical assumptions made by his colleagues, in particular the density assumptions of the near surface snow (or firn). Firn is granular, partially consolidated, accumulated snow older than one year. In its first year, it may also be described as 'neve'. The density of firn can range depending on depth from 200 to 900 kilograms per cubic metre. For the most part, the surface density for East Antarctic firn could be estimated to be approximately 350 kilograms per cubic metre.

The controversy about the state of mass balance in East Antarctica centres on the question of whether firn is rising, or whether ice is rising. This has a massive influence on the outcome of the mass balance determination.

Zwally contends that it is ice, and argues that at the end of the last ice age, roughly 10,000 years ago, the amount of snowfall doubled. This would mean that it has been compacting into solid ice for millennia and continues to do so today. Most other scientists, however, do not agree that this is still going on and argue that any increase in the ice sheet's height is from added snowfall.

A more recent paper (Grazioli et al., 2017) raised questions about the interpretation of satellite-borne radar precipitation measurements as a source of information to cover the entire continent. This paper suggested the need to explicitly monitor and consider snowfall sublimation as an individual term of the ice sheet mass balance. Sublimation is the process of converting solid ice or snow directly to vapour, and sometimes back to solid again.

Zwally et al. (2015) never contradicted climate change proponents, instead claiming to be raising a flag to suggest that rising sea levels may not be caused totally by the melting of Antarctic ice sheets. Some of it may be due to thermal expansion of the oceans. A more recent paper from 2019 by Rignot et al. analysed updated drainage inventory, ice thickness and ice velocity from previous mass balance data to calculate the grounding line ice discharge of 176 basins draining from the ice sheet from 1979 to 2017. Rignot et al. (2019) asserted a more populist view: 'East Antarctica is a major participant in the mass loss from Antarctica … Our observations challenge the traditional view that the East Antarctic Ice Sheet is stable and immune to change.'

Rignot and others (2019) found that the mass loss increased (ignoring margins of error for the moment) from 40 billion tonnes per year in the period 1979 to 1990, to 50 billion tonnes per year in the period 1989 to 2000, to 166 billion tonnes per year in the period 1999 to 2009, then to 252 billion tonnes per year in the period 2009 to 2017. If this last figure is correct, East Antarctica is certainly in a state of negative mass balance and we have much to worry about. However, these newer figures have not yet been verified by satellite observations of gravity and elevation changes.

A study published by a group of 80-plus scientists – the Ice Sheet Mass Balance Inter-Comparison Exercise team – concluded (IMBIE, 2018):

> … between 1992 to 2017, the Antarctic Ice Sheet lost 2,720 billion tonnes of ice, contributing 7.6 mm to global mean sea-level rise. This record of Antarctica mass changes shows that while prior to 2012, Antarctica lost ice at a steady rate of 76 billion tonnes per year, it is now losing ice faster than ever, with more than half of the total ice loss occurring between 2012 and 2017. This increase in ice loss from the continent as a whole is a combination of glacier speed up in West Antarctica and at the Antarctic Peninsula, and reduced growth of the ice sheet in East Antarctica.

The current consensus amongst scientists seems to be that although West Antarctica and the Antarctic Peninsula are losing ice at an increasing rate, the East Antarctic Ice Sheet is growing in mass, but very close to being 'in balance'. It seems that the 35-year-old conclusion in my MSc thesis was not incorrect, just imprecise by today's standards. The greater concern for the world at large is that in coming decades a negative mass balance for East Antarctica may become measurable, particularly if warming continues. If the East Antarctic outlet glaciers start to accelerate, the effect on global sea levels could be significant. Ice sheet contribution to sea-level rise is critical to our understanding of climate change.

A definitive answer requires major innovation in the scientific process, including the ability to continuously monitor and map the entire Antarctic Ice Sheet surface and sub-surface processes. Peters et al. (2021) is an example of potential innovation using passive radar that may provide answers.

Communicating With Antarctica
Decode Section

WYMMA	Please don't worry
WYNNA	Hope you will soon be better
WYSSA	All my (our) love darling
WYTEV	I love you darling
WYTOY	I think about you all the time and hope you are getting along all right
WYVWE	Best love for our anniversary
WYWYE	Merry Christmas and Happy New Year
WYZZA	Please don't wait so long next time
YAAHY	Longing to hear from you again darling
YAANF	How are you darling
YAAWN	Do nothing
YACAS	Shall we endeavour to?
YACIV	Telex mutilated
YADUZ	This is very urgent
YAHEZ	I am (we are) waiting
YAHIB	All are safe and well

YAHOC	Had a party last night to celebrate
YALOG	Decided not to
YANEG	Look after yourself
YARAJ	Have met with an accident
YARJA	Injury is not serious
YASKA	It has been very cold
YIGUM	I have grown a beard which is awful
YIHKE	I have grown a beard which is generally admired
YIHMO	I have grown a beard but think I'll shave it off before I get back to Australia
YIHPY	Hello and how are you?
YIJNO	I have grown a beard
YIKAL	Rather fed up at having to stick around the station/field camp
YIKLA	This is the life!
YILAM	Would be glad of information concerning
YIMOR	Radio reception has been very bad
YINAC	Did not hear your message on Radio Australia
YINAP	The food is first rate and I've put on some weight
YINPA	Glad to hear
YINYV	Leaving the station for a short while don't worry
YISOR	Au revoir
YITUB	I am not sure whether men training dogs or dogs training men
YITWE	Please contact Antarctic Division, Head Office, Kingston, Tasmania, for information about
YITZO	Please send me by relief ship … Kodachromes

YIVYE	Hospitality of people here wonderful
YIZAB	I am setting out on a tractor traverse journey to
YODAK	Waiting arrival of
YOFME	Is (are) making good progress
YOLYX	Would like information about
YONAT	Can afford longer messages
YONTA	I have a thousand questions to ask
YONZZ	Dome C Wilkes Land, a United States summer glaciology research station situated at 74°S, 124°E
YOOAD	Vostok, the Soviet Union's station high on the plateau of inland Antarctica
YOOPZ	Send telex to ship
YOOZK	In reply to your telex my answer is no
YONZF	Gaussberg, an extinct volcano 500 km north-east of Davis on the west of Pazadowsky Bay
YOPCY	Can you tell me
YOPZO	On my return
YORAD	I have been very busy
YOREZ	Please make allowance for
YOSAZ	I have been thinking
YOURD	The Law Dome, an ice dome just over 1000 m high to the south-east of Casey

Antarctic Lingo

AAD	Australian Antarctic Division.
ANARE	Australian National Antarctic Research Expedition.
ARMS	Automatic Remote Magnetic Station.
ATT	A Soviet tank platform used in the Antarctic as a general work vehicle at stations and a prime mover for tractor trains on overland traverses.
Azimuth	Horizontal direction expressed as the angular distance between the direction of a fixed point, such as the observer's heading, and the direction of the object.
Balok	A Soviet sled-mounted living van that consisted of a general living/sleeping/dining area, kitchen, radio room and genset room.
Banya	A Russian sauna or steam bath, and bathhouse.
Bergy bit	Remnant of a broken iceberg around the size of a small cottage.
Big eye	Insomnia caused by being light all day during summer and dark all day during winter.
Blizz line	A permanently connected safety rope stretching from one building or location to another.

CQ	An amateur radio convention to signify 'is anyone listening'.
Declination	Angular distance north or south from the celestial equator measured along a great circle passing through the celestial poles.
Dom	A Russian word for house or building.
Dome C	A polar plateau highpoint located at 74° 44'S, 124° 22'E.
Fast Ice	Sea ice anchored to the shore or bottom of the ocean.
GMT	Greenwich Mean Time is the mean solar time at the Royal Observatory in Greenwich, London when the Sun crosses the Prime Meridian at the Royal Observatory Greenwich.
Growsers	Pads attached to crawler track segments to increase traction.
Growler	A very small remnant of an iceberg (smaller than a bergy bit) less than one metre high above the water and around two metres across.
IAGP	International Antarctic Glaciology Project.
Ice Radar	Radio echo-sounding equipment used to measure ice thickness.
JMR	The brand of satellite doppler receiver (i.e. first-generation global positioning equipment) I used in Antarctica.
Katabatic wind	Downslope wind that forms on the Antarctic plateau due to the action of gravity, typically strengthening during and after sunset.
Kharkovchanka	A special Antarctic traverse vehicle manufactured in the city of Kharkov (now Kharkiv) using the chassis of an ATT with a living van mounted on the tray.

Long eye	A big stare.
Mirny	Means peaceful in Russian and is the name of a Russian coastal Antarctic station.
OIC	Officer in charge (of an Antarctic station).
Polar cap absorption	An effect where high frequency radio signals cannot bounce off the ionosphere to enable communication between operators who are not far enough apart. Also known as PCA.
Polynya	A large area of semi-permanent open water within sea ice.
Polyarnik	A Soviet polar worker.
QSL card	A handwritten postcard sent by amateur radio operators confirming two-way contact by high frequency radio.
Radphone	A radio telephone that was expensive to use, but available for voice communication with loved ones.
SAE	Soviet Antarctic Expedition.
Sastrugi	Rock-hard wave-like features formed by the wind on the snow surface causing erosion of snow.
Shapka	The traditional Russian hat made of fur-lined leather with fold-down ear flaps and an upward folding brim.
Sked'	A pre-programmed time for radio contact or telephone call. A contraction of 'schedule'.
Skip distance	The distance over the Earth's surface between the point where a high frequency radio signal is transmitted, and the point where it is received having travelled to the ionosphere and been refracted back.

Skua	An Antarctic seabird with a reputation for being fierce and aggressive, occasionally sighted deep in the Antarctic interior.
Slushy	The dishwasher for the day who is rostered on duty.
Snow pole	Steel (sometimes bamboo or aluminium) poles placed in the snow to mark a route.
South Geomagnetic Pole	The point at (80° 39'S, 107° 19'E) where the Earth's magnetic field lines split overhead from the day side to the night side.
Tabular iceberg	An iceberg with steep sides and a flat top that has broken off an ice shelf.
Telex	A method of written communication like a telegram, transmitted and received by radio transmission rather than overland wires.
Track Pins	Hardened steel rods that join growser plates on vehicle crawler tracks.
Tractor Train	A diesel-powered crawler-tracked prime mover pulling one or more over-snow sledges.
Vallinke	Russian cold climate boots made from felt.
Vostok	Means 'East' in Russian and is the name of a Russian inland Antarctic station.
Winter (verb)	To spend an entire year at an Antarctic station including the winter season.
Wyssa	(pronounced whizzer and not to confused with the code WYZZA) is both a message and a method of communicating in code between families in Australia and expeditioners in Antarctica. It also means 'All my (our) love darling'.

Author's Publications

Hamley T.C. (1987). 'The East Antarctic Ice from Ice Sheet Flow to Iceberg Dissolution', *University of Melbourne*, Master of Science Thesis.

Hamley, T.C. (1985). 'Glaciological measurements on the 1983-84 Soviet traverse from Mirny to Dome C.' In: T.H. Jacka (ed) *ANARE Research Notes 28*: 180–184.

Hamley, T.C., & Budd, W.F. (1986). 'Antarctic iceberg distribution and dissolution'. *Journal of Glaciology 32*(111):242–251.

Hamley, T.C. (1986). 'Floating Giants' *Australian Natural History Magazine* 22(3) Summer 86-87:112–115

Hamley, T.C. Morgan, V.I. Thwaites, R.J. & Gao, X.Q. (1986). 'An ice core drilling site at Law Dome Summit, Wilkes Land, Antarctica.' *ANARE Research Notes*, 37.

Hamley, T.C., Smith, I.N., & Young, N.W. (1985). 'Mass Balance and ice flow parameters for East Antarctica'. *Journal of Glaciology*, *31*(10), 334–339.

Young, N.W., Sheey, D., & Hamley, T.C. (1982). 'Ice flow along an IAGP flow line, Wilkes Land, Antarctica'. (Abstract) *Annals of Glaciology*, *3*, 346

Bibliography

Amundsen R. (1927). 'My Life as an Explorer'. *William Heinemann Ltd*, London.

Antonello, A. (2018). 'Glaciological Bodies: Australian Visions of the Antarctic Ice Sheet'. *International Review of Environmental History*, *4*(1), 127.

Fretwell, P. et al. (2013). 'Improved ice bed, surface and thickness datasets for Antarctica.' *The Cryosphere*, *7*, 375–393.

Guido, S. (n.d.). 'History of the Antarctic Treaty System'. *Library of Congress*. https://www.loc.gov/ghe/cascade/index.html?appid=eb78cec7f5e34c40a2ee13732c4bf805

Grazioli, J., Madeleine, J.B., Galée, H., Forbes, R., Genthon, C., Krinner, G., & Berne, A. (2017). 'Katabatic winds diminish precipitation contribution to the Antarctic ice mass balance'. *Proceedings of the National Academy of Sciences of the United States of America*, *114*(41), 10858–10863.

Hall, S. (2017). 'What to Believe in Antarctica's Great Ice Debate'. *Scientific American*. www.scientificamerican.com/article/what-to-believe-in-antarctica-rsquo-s-great-ice-debate/

Houlden, J., & Spark, S. (2022). 'Shadowline – The Dunera Diaries of Uwe Radok'. *Monash University Publishing*, 181.

IMBIE team. (2018). 'Mass balance of the Antarctic Ice Sheet from 1992 to 2017'. *Nature, 558*(7709), 219–222.

Jacka, F. & Jacka, E. (1988). 'Mawson's Antarctic Diaries'. *Allen and Unwin*, Sydney, 414.

Jensen, D.C. (2015). 'Mawson's Remarkable Men – the personal stories of the epic 1911-14 Australasian Antarctic Expedition'. *Allen and Unwin*, Sydney, 183.

Lentati, S. (2015). 'The man who cut out his own appendix'. *BBC News magazine*. https://www.bbc.com/news/magazine-32481442

Orheim, O., et al. (2022). 'Antarctic iceberg distribution revealed through three decades of systemic ship-based observations'. *Journal of Glaciology*, 1–15. https://doi.org/10.1017/jog.2022.84

Parkinson, C. (2014). 'Global Sea Ice Coverage from Satellite data: Annual Cycle and 35 yr trends'. Journal of Climate, *27*(24), 9377–9382.

Parkinson, C. (2019). 'A 40-y record reveals gradual Antarctic sea ice increases followed by decreases at rates far exceeding the rates seen in the Arctic'. *Proceedings of the National Academy of Sciences of the United States of America, 116*(29), 14414–14423.

Peters, S.T., et al. (2021). 'Glaciological Monitoring using the sun as a radio source for Echo Detection'. *Geophysical Research Letters, 48*(14). https://doi.org/10.1029/2021GL092450

Radok, U. (1985). 'The Antarctic Ice'. *Scientific American, 253*(2), 98–105.

Rignot, E., et al. (2019). 'Four decades of Antarctic Ice Sheet Mass Balance from 1979-2017'. *Proceedings of the National Academy of Sciences of the United States of America, 116*, 1095–1103.

Rogosov, V. & Bermel, N. (2009). 'Auto-appendectomy in the Antarctic: case report', *British Medical Journal*. https://doi.org/10.1136/bmj.b4965

Sancton, J. (2021). 'Madhouse at the end of the Earth – The Belgica's Journey into the Dark Antarctic Night', *WH Allen*, London, 350.

Scambos, T. & Shuman C. (2016). 'Comment on 'Mass gains of Antarctic ice sheet exceed Losses' by H.J. Zwally and others' *Journal of Glaciology, 62*(233), 599–603.

Zwally J. and others. (2015). 'Mass Gains of Antarctic ice sheet exceed Losses'. *Journal of Glaciology, 61*(230), 1019–1036.